Inside the Darkness

A Walk Through Grief

Cathy Wilhelm

Cathy Wilhelm
10/27/15

ISBN: 1-4499-1196-X
ISBN-13: 9781449911966

Dedication

To my daughter, Christy,

and the friends who held my hand.

Table of Contents

Introduction

Grief touches virtually every life. It has to do with an emotional response to a loss. We can lose a dream, a goal, a boyfriend or girlfriend, and more. Cathy Wilhelm writes about grief brought about by the death of her beloved husband Tom.

It has been my privilege to walk the path of grief with many parishioners, family, and friends mainly over the span of my fifty-two years of ministry. This journey has had the guidance of two pioneers in grief ministry-Granger Westberg and Elizabeth Kubler-Ross.

Although there are stages in grieving, they are not always in the same order for everyone and the journey is unique to each individual. Never was this truer than in my ministry to the author of this book, Cathy Wilhelm.

As this book will clearly reveal, Cathy has a heightened emotional sensitivity and also the ability to express herself with hard-hitting honesty. She is not content with many of the clichés of well-meaning people. She will not stuff and bury what she feels only to have come back and bite her when she least expects. She accepted from me the common sense counsel of regular exercise, nutritious meals, spiritual input, making time for nourishing people, and avoiding like the plague people she finds to be toxic.

Many of us blunt our pain in a variety of ways that do not lead to health. Cathy Wilhelm invites you to feel the full intensity of your pain and journey with God and the people who love you. She knows first-hand that God is big enough to handle her anger.

Praise God for the people who are there for you however bumpy the road and however long the trail. We celebrate the God in Christ Who walked the path of sorrow before us and now walks with us in our pain and loneliness and anger and more.

Now I invite you to walk with Cathy in all of her intensity and honest expressions. May something of her journey enable you to be there for others and to honestly and upfront and personal deal with your own losses.

Shalom.

Arne Walker, Pastor and Spiritual Director for the author, residing in Gatlinburg, TN

Preface

Although we have never met, if you are dealing with the loss of a loved one we share a unique experience called grief. With the loss of both parents I thought I understood sorrow, but the night my husband suffered a fatal heart attack I was proved wrong. His sudden death propelled me headlong into grief, the dark tunnel known only to others who have walked through it.

Grief is not neat. It is a violent, relentless storm pounding your world and, while means of expression differ with individual personalities, its pain is universal. Healing comes in tiny increments as you find the courage to keep walking and rebuild your life.

This book, compiled of journal entries from my walk through grief, is my attempt to bring hope and comfort to others struggling with loss. The intense pain you feel and the sensation of being lost in your own life are normal elements of grief. After all, you have suffered a devastating blow much like a tsunami slamming into your life, and all you can do is hold on till the storm passes and waves subside. As you begin to rebuild I wish I could tell you that in "X" amount of time, if you follow certain guidelines, things will get better. Unfortunately, grief is as individual as a fingerprint and different for everyone, a journey with no road maps or speed limits. Be gentle with yourself. Don't try to rush the process. Don't be discouraged when healing doesn't come in a month, six months, a year, or more.

I've heard someone say of a widow, "She is doing really well," and I wonder how they can tell. Does she cry only in private? Does she say, "Fine," when someone asks, "How are you?" Does she bury the grief and try to smile through her pain? Observers must have thought I was not doing well when I burst into tears for no reason or said, "Crummy," when asked how I was doing. Personality dictates the way we react to grief but, even masked, the pain is no less intense.

Grieving is hard work, and in the beginning it affects your physical health. Whenever I thought of tomorrow without Tom, or the next day, or the next, fear crippled me. I burst into tears without warning, sobbing until my heart hurt and I could not catch my breath. I felt weak and had no energy to do basic chores. I was exhausted all the time—mentally, physically, and emotionally—but could never sleep more than an hour or two. I had no appetite and lost 16 pounds in the first three weeks. Unable to concentrate I could not read the paper with comprehension or remember simple instructions. Driving home from work I drove past the road I had turned on every day for twenty-five years. I felt hollow inside and although I went places, did things, and talked to people, nothing was real. It was as if I had died too, yet kept breathing.

I stumbled onto a book, *A Grief Observed,* by C. S. Lewis, which was his journal of grief after the death of his wife. The raw emotion and agony he expressed consoled me. It was as if Lewis took my hand, walked with me through the dark maze, and helped me understand the ravages of grief. The comfort his writing offered inspired me to write my own grief story, hoping it too would help someone shattered by loss. Lewis became my mentor. I found an online study with a college professor in Wisconsin that covered two of his books: *A Grief Observed* and *The Problem of Pain*. Through candid dialogue we explored the depths of sorrow and pain and I was able to turn a corner and began to absorb my loss. Later, I started a Bible study with a group from my church using books by Lewis and we continue to meet monthly.

I hung birdfeeders in the backyard and discovered a passion for bird watching. Bluebirds are my obsession, and I watched three broods being raised in the house I put up for them outside my sunroom window.

I knew nothing about landscaping but I planted yellow roses and black-eyed-susans in the backyard. The morning I looked out and spotted the first tiny rosebud with just a tinge of yellow peeping out, I sensed life slipping back in.

All these things are pieces of my new life but make no mistake, I have not, nor ever will "get over" losing my husband. Tom was my best friend, my lover, my partner in everything, and the one I planned to grow old with. I can't bury my head in the sand and pretend things are fine. That's not real. Somehow I must walk through this storm and not let it destroy me. I never thought I could find the way back when my world turned black that night, and even after 5 years I still have difficult days. I think about Tom 24/7 and miss him terribly, but I am learning to accept the loss and cherish the memories. I still cry, although not every day, and I have days when I need help from my friends; nevertheless, I now find joy in the good things left in my life. Someone recently told me she was jealous of me because I had so many friends. Imagine that! Someone envies a widow's life. Friends cannot take Tom's place but their support helps me keep walking and reminds me I am not alone. I can't give you a formula for healing or answers to the whys that torture a survivor's mind, but I can help you remember you still have a life to live and a purpose. Hold on to Jesus until He shows you the next step and know He is just a whisper away when the sorrow begins to swallow you.

Cathy Wilhelm

chapter I
Thrust Into Darkness

"TOM! ARE YOU ok? Tom! Tom! TOM!" Gasping for breath, Tom couldn't say anything but his desperate look begged me for help, and then seconds later it faded into a blank stare as his lifeless body melted into the chair. Trembling in the eerie stillness, I dialed 9-1-1. "Please send an ambulance!" I pleaded, "I think my husband has had a heart attack!"

❧

Monday evening, November 24, 2003

Tom and I have a nightly routine; we carry our coffee to the living room, sink down into our "dual" recliners, and watch Jeopardy. Tonight, with Thanksgiving just three days away I stacked cookbooks beside my chair so we could plan this year's menu. I started scanning recipes and if something sounded good I read the ingredients to Tom during commercials to get his approval.

"Maybe I'll make chocolate cake this year," I said, "since all the kids like it."

"No, you'd better make something else," Tom said heading for the kitchen.

Knowing Tom was diabetic and trying to be careful about desserts I started to consider an alternative. Just then, he walked back into the room munching on a chocolate chip cookie. "Well," I said picking at him, "why not have chocolate cake if you're going to eat cookies anyway?"

"I can resist cookies," he said, "but not your chocolate cake. I'd eat the whole thing."

Those were the last words we ever said to each other.

Tom coughed.

"You ok?" I asked, still focused on my recipe. When Tom didn't respond I glanced over at him and he seemed to be choking. "Tom!" I jumped up to help him but could only stand powerless in front of him and watch...

"Is he breathing?" the operator asked.

"No."

"You're OK," she reassured me, "The paramedics are on the way. Are you willing to try CPR?"

"Yes! But I don't know how."

Shaking, I tried to follow her instructions. I pulled Tom's limp body from the recliner onto the floor and turned him over. Cold waves washed over me when I noticed his face already had a blue tint. I knelt beside him, tilted his head, and lifted his chin, but maneuvering his lifeless body was like working with two hundred and twenty-five pounds of dough. I tried to hold his tongue back but his chin kept slipping. "I need more hands!" Frantic,

I tossed the phone aside and tried to breathe for him. I could feel Tom slipping away from me.

"Jesus, help me!" I screamed in a voice that sounded strange and distant. It was as if someone else said it, not me. Following the operator's instructions, I changed positions after a few breaths and began a pumping motion on Tom's chest. Then, a burst of air rushed from his body and fear and disbelief paralyzed me. I knew it was his last breath.

"Was that him?" the operator asked.

"Yes," I told her as the phone dropped. Outside I could see flashing lights as a team of paramedics bolted into the room straight to Tom. The attending policeman ushered me out of the room while they shocked Tom's heart and started an IV, but it was too late. Too late.

As the paramedics loaded Tom into the ambulance I studied a few seconds about what I would tell Christy and Tammy, and then I dialed the phone. Neither was prepared for the news I had to deliver. Tammy had called just five minutes earlier from the grocery store to ask what she could bring for Thanksgiving and she was still shopping when I called.

"Did you think of something I could bring?" she asked.

"No," I said trying to be calm, "I called to let you know Tom had a heart attack and they're taking him to the hospital by ambulance."

"Oh no!" Tammy said.

When I reached Christy, she was just getting home from the hospital where she had spent the day with her biological father near death battling cancer. Even though my heart knew Tom was dead, I could not be the one to rip him from their lives. Besides, the paramedics were still working on Tom when they carried him to the ambulance and nobody had said that awful word—yet. I repeated the message to Christy and told her to meet me in the emergency room.

The ambulance pulled away and everyone left except the police officer who had stayed close to me ever since he came on the scene.

"Thank you," I said walking toward the front door. "You can go now. I'm OK, and I can drive myself to the hospital. I just need to find my shoes."

The officer refused to leave. "Go ahead and get your shoes," he said, "then I'll take you to the hospital."

"But I'll need my car to get back home," I reasoned.

"Don't worry," he insisted, "I'll bring you back home."

I could see my arguments were not about to change his mind so I gave in and went to find my shoes.

In those minutes before we left I didn't cry or get hysterical. Instead, I was consumed with rage. I was angry with God. Jesus came tonight when I screamed for His help. I felt Him there. But He didn't stop Tom from dying.

"Why? Why? Why?" I prayed, begging God for answers. "Why didn't You help us? Why did you take Tom away from me? Why?"

He didn't answer.

"So, You didn't love me after all," I said. And then we left.

Christy and Tammy barely made it to the emergency room when someone came to lead us to a private room where the doctor would meet with us.

"This can't be good," Tammy said.

Seconds after we sat down the doctor came in and said the words...Tom was gone. Then he led us to where Tom lay so we could say our last goodbye.

"This can't be happening," Tammy said, burying her face in her husband David's chest.

I touched Tom, straightened his hair, kissed his face, and then slowly turned toward the door, but it was hard to leave him. In the emergency room Tom's blood had been pumped artificially and even though he never revived his skin was warm now and his color back to normal.

"How can he be dead?" I thought to myself, "when he looks so perfect." I wanted to believe this was all a mistake and Tom was still alive, but then I remembered I saw his last breath.

"I was prepared to lose the other one," Christy whispered as we walked out together, "but not Tom."

လ∞ဢ

Tom was diagnosed with Type II diabetes in 1989 during a routine physical examination and afterwards, he saw the doctor regularly. His blood sugar was under control with insulin and healthy eating habits and there had been no complications from the disease. Then a few months ago, Tom went in for his annual check-up and the doctor detected a slight abnormality in his electrocardiogram and suggested a stress test just as a precaution. Worried that Tom wasn't telling me everything, I bombarded him with questions, and he promised me it was just a standard procedure. Since the doctor waited two months to schedule the stress test, I felt more at ease. Surely, if he thought it was serious he would have taken immediate action.

The stress test took two days and Tom was able to complete it with no trouble; however, the physician reading his report noticed there was again a slight irregularity. He told Tom he didn't think there was any reason for alarm but wanted to set up a dye test at the hospital just to be sure. Should there be a blockage, a stent could be inserted in his heart immediately—a simple procedure requiring only one night in the hospital. We were cautious but not panicked, since there was still no immediate action taken. The dye test wasn't scheduled until a few weeks later.

On Wednesday, October 29, 2003, at eight a.m., Tom checked into the hospital for the dye test, which took about an hour. Fear brushed over me when the doctor came out with a long face and told us they had found a blockage. Tom was transported into surgery where two stents were inserted to open his artery and he was admitted to the Cardiac Care Unit. Everything went as expected and Tom was released the next morning. His doctor told us there was no recuperation for the heart, but Tom needed to be careful not to break open the incision. He should not drive or lift anything for ten days and he could not return to work until he came back for his follow-up visit. The nurse handed him a list of prescriptions and guidelines to follow.

For the next week Tom enjoyed our new sunroom. He watched birds, read a Zane Gray Western, and listened to *The Fabulous Fifties* CD collection. Eleven days later on Monday, November 10, 2003, Tom had his return visit to the doctor and was released to go back to work. His heart sounded good and the doctor instructed him to follow a low-cholesterol diet and begin walking daily. We breathed a sigh of relief, as Tom went back to work and life was normal again.

Rather than walk outside with winter coming, Tom decided to buy a treadmill and set it up in the computer room. The doctor told him to begin with a quarter mile then gradually build up to two miles a day. On Thursday night, November 20, 2003, Tom walked a quarter mile, which was five minutes on the treadmill. Friday he walked seven, and each following day he added a few minutes. By Monday, November 24, 2003, Tom was up to walking for thirteen minutes, but he came out of the room sweating afterwards. I fussed at him for pushing too hard and got mad at myself for not being back there with him to make him stop. Tom, impatient and hardworking, only knew one speed—wide open. He wanted to get well, and he wanted to do it now.

Tom sat down at the table and checked his blood pressure, which was elevated a bit, then poured himself a cup of coffee and came into the living room to watch Jeopardy. We enjoyed a normal, happy, full day. And then, he was gone...

⇢⇦

Minutes after we returned home, the hospital called to ask me to donate Tom's organs. Now I understood why they kept his blood circulating when they knew he wouldn't make it. Tom and I had never discussed organ donation and at that moment I could not imagine them cutting him open. I knew Tom was dead, and yet I could not make the fact my reality. I just said, "No, I'm sorry, I can't," and hung up.

It was late as I stood in the kitchen trying to absorb what I had just witnessed. Tom was not coming home and now we needed to call friends and family with the bad news. I heard myself say, "Tom died," and everyone believed me. But it was not yet real to me. The first call I made was to Debbie.

"Oh no!" she said, jolted by the news. "Do you want me to come over?"

My voice said, "No, you don't need to," but my heart was screaming, "YES!" and wondering why I told her not to come. Debbie heard my silent plea and came anyway bringing our friend Brenda with her.

Tom and I became friends with Debbie and Santo, and Brenda and Jerry in 1992 when we joined their church. Through the years we visited, enjoyed dinners at each other's home, and even went on a vacation together the year before Tom died. After Tom's stent surgery, Brenda made dinner for the gang and we had so much fun we planned another evening together the next month, but Tom died before we could go.

Next, I called my boss to tell him I wouldn't be in the next day. "Mike?" I asked when he answered.

"Yes," he said.

"I won't be able to work the rest of the week," I said then paused for a moment, "Tom died tonight."

"Your Tom!" Mike asked.

"Yes," I sighed.

"Oh no!" he said and we both held the phone in silence a few seconds. "Let me pray with you." In a soft voice Mike prayed for me over the phone and I clung to every word for hope.

"Thank you," I said.

Afterwards, I felt too weak to make another call so I asked Christy, Tammy, and David to contact the others. Stunned by the news most responded by saying, "I just saw Tom and he felt great."

In spite of the late hour several friends came to be with us, and I repeated the details of Tom's death to each one. Maybe soon I would be able to grasp the reality I described.

After a while everyone left, everyone except Christy.

చ∽ఆ

Christy was four years old when we married Tom. I say, "We," because Christy told everyone she met, "Me and Mommy are marrying Tom." She was crazy about him and looked forward to our dates as much as I did. Tom courted us both and always gave Christy special attention when he came over. Ours was a second marriage for both and Tom brought with him two young teenagers, John and Tammy. Tom was the best daddy I'd ever met and for twenty-five years he was Christy's.

Christy has Tom's wit, and oftentimes she comments the way he would about a situation and with the same sly grin. One day we had lunch at Arby's and when Christy ordered a Big Montana I knew she was thinking of Tom.

"That's the sandwich Tom always ordered," I said.

"I know," Christy said, "except he called it the Big Mountaineer."

Christy knew I was having a hard day and, like Tom, tried to find something positive to say to make it better.

"You have a lot of things going for you," Christy said. "You're healthy and look younger than your age."

"Now you sound like Tom," I said.

Christy stayed with me day and night the week Tom died and her presence soothed me in a way nothing else could. She had grown up watching the love between Tom and me and now more than anyone else she understood the depth of my loss.

Although life stopped for me, the world kept turning and everyone else went back to business as usual. Christy had a job and needed to go back home and resume her daily routine. Since she couldn't be with me all the time she called every day, sometimes several times a day. If I didn't answer at home she called my cell phone, and if I didn't answer it she looked for me. Christy needed to know I was OK and I needed to know she was close. Without Tom I had nobody to check in with. Who would know about my life now, whether I came home or not? Christy's calls eased my loneliness and the dazed feeling of being disconnected from life.

Weeks turned into months, and now years, and Christy is still close by. She and I spend a day together every week or so to see a movie, walk the mall, or browse Sam's Club to sample new products. On really tough days – birthdays, anniversaries, holidays, and especially Thanksgiving—she makes sure I'm not alone. I never thought I could manage another Thanksgiving dinner, but Christy spends the day with me and we cook it together. It's our new tradition, like watching *Jesus Christ Superstar* every Easter. We started a weekly Bible study and, even though Christy doesn't share my love for the writings of C. S. Lewis, she struggled through *The Screwtape Letters* anyway because it is my favorite book. It doesn't matter what we do, I just need to know she's there – still near when my day gets too sad.

Wednesday, November 26, 2003 – 2 days later

Kathy stopped by to see me at ten a.m. and even though it was late morning I was not dressed yet. I answered the door wearing my nightgown and, worse yet, I didn't even care. Neither did Kathy.

I met Kathy three years ago when Tom and I joined the Lutheran Church and our friendship came easy, since we are close in age and have similar backgrounds. Her visit was a nice surprise that gave me someone to help make sense of what happened. We sat in the sunroom and I reconstructed the details of Tom's death for my friend. Kathy seemed to understand my pain and even the anger, having lost a close friend to cancer.

"I tried to perform CPR on Tom," I said "but I couldn't save him."

"I used to be a CPR instructor," Kathy said, "and statistics show the percentage of people who are brought back or saved with CPR is pretty low, less than twenty percent."

"Really?" I asked, "On television it always works."

While we were still discussing CPR, my cousin Graham, a Police Officer, came to the door dressed in his uniform. It always startles the neighbors when Graham pulls his patrol car into the driveway, but he just comes by to check on me. After I introduced him to Kathy I asked Graham to join us in the sunroom.

Kathy went on explaining CPR to me, helping ease the guilt I felt for Tom's death, and Graham supported her comments.

"I have performed CPR on nine people," Graham said, "and have not been able to save one of them."

Their words were balm for my spirit and quieted the accuser in my head for a few minutes.

❧❧

I was tormented for months every time I relived my botched attempt at CPR, because I believed if I had known how to perform CPR properly I could have saved Tom. Whenever the guilt overwhelmed me, I called Kathy and she quoted the statistics to me. She didn't care how many times I asked, she just told me again.

Even though I could not go back to church right away, Kathy called every week. Then when I did go back she stood beside me and held my hand the first time I took communion without Tom. I cried and she cried with me. We always cried together—on the phone, at the movies, and even in restaurants—because as Kathy says, "We are both sappy."

Other than Thanksgiving week, my toughest day is September second, our wedding anniversary. I was at work on the first anniversary I spent without Tom, and a beautiful basket of flowers with a little pink bird sitting atop was delivered to our office with my name on it. I cried when I opened the card and saw it was from Kathy, but this time they were not all sad tears.

❧❧

Graham continues to stop by now and then to check on me when he is cruising in the morning, and it makes me feel safe knowing he is watching out for me.

Thursday, November 27, 2003 – 3 days later, Thanksgiving Day

As a rule, Thanksgiving is the day I look at my life and pick out the good things, knowing I am blessed regardless of my circumstances. Today, rather than a sense of well-being, fear hovers overhead like a dark cloud haunting me with "what ifs." Tom's love was my safe place and without him I can't think about tomorrow. What if I get sick, lose my job, wreck the car, et cetera? I have zero control over my life and it scares me.

Christy and I were alone today with nothing pressing to do, no decisions to make, no people to call, and no places we had to be. Realizing the negative impact a Thanksgiving Day funeral could have on future celebrations, I deliberately postponed all of Tom's services until after the holiday.

The fridge is packed with food that friends have brought in the past two days, but it is Thanksgiving and we need a diversion from the sorrow. Christy and I got dressed and went out for lunch. We had just walked through the door at Ryan's Buffet Restaurant when a young man spotted us, came running over, and gave us both a bear hug. It was Robbie. The grin on his face said he was happy to see us.

Robbie worked with Tom and, since he moved here from another state and had no family close by, Tom was like a father to him. Several other coworkers had told us Robbie was inconsolable when he heard the news about Tom.

We stood in the entry way for a few minutes listening to Robbie's stories about Tom and crying with him. His words were more important to us than a turkey dinner, and his hug more nourishing. I was thankful.

෧෧

The entire week of Thanksgiving is a dark memory for me now. Autumn hues are catalysts of pain. When I see houses and businesses adorned with seasonal decorations—pumpkins, turkeys, or fall scenes—I start to sink. Tom died on Monday before Thanksgiving and the next two days were consumed with making funeral arrangements and calling relatives. On Friday we received friends at the funeral home, and Tom's service was on Saturday, followed by interment. Thanksgiving will never be the same.

Saturday, November 29, 2003 – 5 days later

It was cold today as we made our way to the chairs by Tom's grave with friends and family huddled close behind us.

"This is it," I told myself, "the final step. I have no more people to call, appointments to keep, or plans to make. Now what? What do I do with the rest of my life?"

The past few days had been so hectic planning the funeral I didn't have time to stop and think, but now it was finished. I felt panic begin to set in. Then I looked up and saw Mike and Bruce standing in front of me a few yards away. I couldn't remember the words of Mike's prayer over the phone Monday night, but I hadn't forgotten how much it helped me. I felt the same strength today when I looked up and saw them standing close by, an anchor in my storm. Their presence helped me to focus on the one thing I will do after this day is over. I will go back to work on Monday, and for now that is enough.

The service went just as I'd hoped and several people commented about how well it captured who Tom was. Flowers adorned the front of the chapel. The yellow roses I bought stood beside the casket, and one long-stemmed yellow rose lay on Tom's chest where I'd placed it. A single yellow rose was Tom's special way of saying, "I love you." Sometimes, when he knew I'd had a bad day, Tom drove by my work and left one yellow rose in my car, but most of the time he gave me one for no reason at all. Today I left one for him.

The funeral service was important to me and I wanted it to be a special goodbye to Tom. Each song and

Scripture was part of Tom's story and every person I asked to participate said, "Yes," without hesitation. His friend Jerry talked about the kind of friend Tom was and read a poem that was just right. Tom wanted me to play *Come What May*, our wedding song, at his funeral and although the words made me cry it helped me most of all. The line, *"For as long as I'm living, I'm living only for you,"* was a reminder Tom loved me every minute until the second he left. When Lydia sang *Thank You* at the end, I felt Tom walk into Heaven and for those few moments I had perfect peace.

Jerry stood beside me as everyone filed out, and by the time I walked out the chapel was nearly empty. Outside the door my friend Barbra was waiting to give me a hug before we made our way to the gravesite. The love and support I felt today from everyone there made me think about the previous few days of preparation and planning when so many came to help...My sister Peggy took off work to stay at my house in case anyone called or came by while Christy, Tammy, and I went to order flowers and make the arrangements. My friend Angie popped in at the funeral home to give me a hug when she drove by and noticed my car parked outside. Friends brought food to the house, sent flowers, cards, and gifts. Tom's sister Marcia stood beside me at the funeral home when we received friends so I wouldn't feel alone, and then for three and a half hours people filed by the casket to express their sorrow and offer sympathy. As I listened to stories about Tom, some from folks I had never met, I kept wishing he could know how much he was loved.

Once everyone had gathered at Tom's grave Pastor Walker offered a prayer and then the veterans performed a brief military service including a twenty-one-gun salute. Tom's son John, a United States Naval officer, looked so handsome sitting there in his dress uniform. Customarily, the veterans fold the flag draped over the casket and present it to the widow, but I asked them to give it to John instead. When I heard the veteran's words as he placed the flag in John's hands I was so proud of both father and son. John stood to salute his dad as the rifles fired and I felt the love between them. Our goodbye was perfect and I knew it would have made Tom smile.

ॐॐ

John stayed another week after his family returned to Hawaii to help me finish some things Tom had left undone. John was fifteen when Tom and I married and now at forty he is much like his dad in appearance, voice, and mannerisms. John joined the Navy after high school and through hard work he gained advancement from enlisted man to Officer. He had been stationed in California for most of his Navy career but was transferred to Hawaii a few months before Tom died.

Tom had worked hard on our sunroom addition but he died before he could complete the finishing touches. Two ceiling fan/light combinations were still in boxes on the floor, and the outside walls had a layer of primer but needed a final coat of paint. John borrowed some of his dad's old clothes and went to work where Tom left off, and by the end of the week the project was complete.

John's presence comforts me in a special way. He is part of Tom, and we not only share our grief but also our memories. Tom's death doesn't seem real, it can't be real, and yet it is. Having John here gives me a few more days to take in what has happened before I have to start this new life without Tom.

Saturday, December 13, 2003 – 19 days later

Today, for the first time I feel the full impact of losing Tom. Since his death I have not been left alone until now. Christy stayed with me until John came in from Hawaii. Chatter filled the house when out-of-town guests who came for the funeral gathered here to reminisce. Now everyone has gone home to resume a normal life. Walking slowly through my empty house in the deafening silence, I know for me "normal" no longer exists.

The bar is covered with food and the fridge is packed with leftovers from meals delivered during the week by caring friends. Tom's first issue of *Bass Fishing* tops the pile of unopened mail on the dining room table. He'd just bought a used boat and planned to do a lot of fishing come spring. Near the phone is a note Tom scribbled on a scrap of paper. That handwriting! How we laughed about it all these years. Now it is gold to me, so personal, so much a part of him. Clutching the note I feel the loss again. I can't comprehend this new existence.

Desperate to hold onto Tom, nothing is more important than the cards and letters he gave me through the years, now tucked away in drawers. Going room to room I searched relentlessly until I found them all. One envelope contained five letters Tom had written to me in 1993 while I was in Nashville. I spent ten days there sitting with my dad at St. Thomas Hospital where he was undergoing brain surgery. Tom wanted to do something special to show how much he loved and missed me. Because we could not afford to send flowers, he wrote me a love letter every day and surprised me with them when I came home. Tom was not a writer but he knew how much I love letters. It was the best gift he ever gave me. I emptied out our fireproof lock-box to make room for my treasure. I sat down in my chair and read each one over and over, straining through the tears.

I put the letters away and walked down into the basement, Tom's woodworking shop. Patterns and materials are stacked beside his unfinished project, the shelf for our new sunroom. Our new sunroom...the addition we built together for our twenty-fifth wedding anniversary gift to each other, so beautiful, yet I cannot bear to walk into it. Overwhelmed by loneliness, I just sat on the basement steps sobbing.

&~&

Tom and I had worked together for the past few years remodeling rooms in our house, and this year we decided to add a sunroom to celebrate our twenty-fifth wedding anniversary. It took about two months to complete the project and we bought wicker furniture and a small dining table with four chairs to complement it. Tom and I loved the new addition and ate supper at our new table every night for the next few weeks. We planned to do some serious bird watching and hung several feeders outside the window, including one for goldfinches. The chair by the window offered the best view so we teased each other about who got to sit there.

"We'll have to get a whistle," Tom said, "and blow it every ten minutes so we can swap places."

We didn't get a chance to implement the ten-minute system because Tom died one month after we finished the sunroom.

After Tom's death every time I walked into the sunroom I felt like I was smothering. The grief overwhelmed me. I stopped feeding the birds, and in my heart dared them to come back. I did not want life to go on because it had not gone on for Tom and me.

In a few weeks I decided to make a scrapbook of Tom and needed a place to spread the pictures out where I could leave them until I was finished. The sunroom was the perfect place, but I still only went out there if I wanted to work on the book.

Eleven months after Tom died, Brenda and Jerry lost their teenage son in a camping accident. A few months later Brenda asked Debbie and me to enroll in a quilting class with her. Neither Debbie nor I wanted to, but we signed up anyway because we felt it might help Brenda deal with her grief. As it turned out, quilting was not that easy and it took all three of us putting our heads together to remember the process.

Brenda's mother, known for her unique philosophy, once said, "Two heads are better than one, even if one of them is a goat head." Thus we became "The Goatheads."

We found it easier to work on our quilts if we did it together, and in order to do that we needed space for a cutting table and three sewing machines. The sunroom met all of the requirements, so we began meeting here every Tuesday night for quilting. Not only is it good therapy but we now have three handmade quilts.

I seldom go into the sunroom unless I'm with someone, but it has proven to be a good meeting place. In addition to quilting I have used it for Bible studies and our family Christmas parties.

In March, four months after Tom died, I decided to invite the birds back. I filled the finch feeder and hung it back on the same limb, wondering if they would return. The next morning I looked out the window and counted eighteen goldfinches on and around the feeder. It was as if my world had been on hold waiting until I was ready to come back.

I think I heard God whisper, "See, there is still life out here."

The world is a scary place without Tom. If I think about the future I can't cope, but then I remember Tom's words to me in a card when I was overburdened with caring for my ailing parents, "One day is all you need to face."

All those goldfinches would have thrilled Tom. In fact, he would have taken their picture.

෬෬෬

God used birds to draw me back into life. One Saturday morning I counted seventeen different kinds of birds in my back yard within the span of an hour. Among the mix was a towhee that appeared to do the hokey pokey when he scratched for food. Hummingbirds dive-bombed each other to protect their spot on the feeder, and a nuthatch walked head first down the hickory tree. A red-bellied woodpecker hung up-side-down on the suet feeder nearby, while the bluebird couple investigated the house I had put up. Later that evening I watched them move in.

Watching the birds showed God's provision to me and helped me see the bigger picture. One evening when I was driving home just before dusk, I looked out my front passenger window and saw an owl gliding beside my car. He flew with me for about a hundred yards before disappearing into the trees. It was a breath-taking experience and my spirit heard the Lord softly say, "I am with you."

Monday, December 15, 2003 – 21 days later

Tonight I dozed in the recliner. When I woke up and saw Tom wasn't in his chair I thought he must have gone on to bed. Then full consciousness yanked me back into the real world. Tom died. He's gone – gone. I felt the cold waves again with the rush of fear and sick hollowness that plagues my every waking moment, the weight I cannot put down.

After three weeks it still doesn't seem real. I cannot absorb what has happened. This morning the alarm sounded and for a second, until I was fully awake, life was normal. And then, the cold wave...Tom wasn't there to hit snooze for seven more minutes, or hold me until time to get up. He won't make coffee while I shower or sit with me to read the paper and chat over breakfast. As creatures of habit, morning after morning our routine was the same, and now memories of those simple acts cause the deepest pain. They bring the harsh reminder that today, and every day, I will be alone.

I feel lost. I live in my house, drive my car, but someone has stolen my life. I don't want to get up or ever walk out the door again. I can't face another day, except I have no choice; I have a job, a house, and a family. So I take a deep breath, put one foot in front of the other, and take another step. When I walk through the door I go over the daily message I give myself, "Tom is happy in Heaven, but your life isn't finished yet."

Tuesday, December 16, 2003 – 22 days later

Peggy came over tonight with a plate of goodies from the Christmas party she had been to with her friends. She gets together every year with a group of women that have known each other since high school. She invited me to come along this year thinking it would be good for me to get out of the house, but I couldn't.

I appreciate people asking me to participate in their holiday plans, because I know they care and want to help. But they have not been where I am now and cannot know the sheer torture of holidays during the first year of grief. Even happy memories bombard my heart and press me to the ground with sorrow. This year and for as long as I live, Tom will not be here for Christmas. I need time to absorb that.

When Peggy got here I was a wreck. I had been alone all day in the house Tom and I shared and the memories we made were crushing me. I didn't want to eat but I was glad my sister brought food, because she came with it and I needed someone to come.

ॐॐ

Holidays that first year without Tom were dreadful, and during the four weeks between Thanksgiving and Christmas it seemed I had stepped in quicksand and kept sinking day by day. I wanted to close my eyes until the commercials stopped, the parties ended, and the pain dissipated. I wasn't sure I could survive Christmas this year – or if I wanted to.

Tom's boss invited me to the company Christmas party, and I knew Tom would have wanted me to go. Knowing how difficult it would be for me to go without Tom, he also invited Christy. Tom and I always shop early, so he had bought his present for the gift exchange before he died. Everyone agreed that whoever had Tom's name would buy a present for me.

Tom was close with his co-workers and I felt their love for him that night, as everyone rallied around Christy and me. An Elvis impersonator was hired to entertain the group at the party and he strolled over by me when he sang *Teddy Bear*. Tom's friends knew I loved Elvis as a teenager, and I appreciated their gesture to cheer me up. After the song, "Elvis" presented me with a giant purple Share Bear. It was a gift from the group to say, "We are crying too." I cried throughout the party, but by this time I was sobbing out of control and had to leave. Their gift helped me, and for the next year Share Bear sat on my couch to keep me company.

My bosses always take us out for lunch on Christmas Eve, and then we take the rest of the day off. They knew how much I loved Red Lobster last year, so we went there again. As soon as I walked into the restaurant I felt my chest tighten, and then the hostess seated us at the same table where we had sat the previous year. I looked up at the same people who had surrounded the table last year, except one. Tom's absence was screaming at me and it felt like I was choking. I didn't think I could make it through the meal, but Mike and Bruce started talking and lightened the mood a bit. Still, I was glad when we left.

"Let's go somewhere else next year," I suggested.

Wednesday, December 17, 2003 – 23 days later

This morning when I came to work Mike was in a project meeting with Jim, one of the Structural Engineers that works closely with our office. Other than answering his calls at work, I knew very little about Jim and had met him only once. That's why it took me by surprise when he stopped by my desk on the way out after the meeting. He stood quietly beside my chair for a few seconds and I sensed he wanted to say something. These days everyone tries to say things to help me. Some quote scripture, others remind me of the twenty-five happy years I had with Tom or tell me he is happy in Heaven. All good, all true, and yet none hold any comfort for me now – almost nothing does.

"How are you doing?" Jim asked.

"OK," I said. It wasn't true, but I reserve "crummy" for those who really know me. I waited for him to offer more of the "tried and true" condolences I'd come to expect.

Jim paused for a moment. "I lost my dad when I was fourteen," he said speaking very softly. "He was working at the Alcoa Aluminum Plant and had just gotten his lunch out and opened his sandwich to eat when he fell out of his chair. He was gone, and he was just forty-four years old."

Watching Jim's expression as he described the sudden loss of his dad, I could feel his brokenness. Something was different this time, his compassion was real. Jim knew this pain.

"Paramedics were on the scene immediately," he continued, "but they couldn't save him."

Jim told me about the struggles in his family after his dad's death. His mom didn't have a job at the time and was left with three kids. Jim had two sisters, one ready to graduate high school, and the other just thirteen.

"Everything changed that day," Jim said, "and it was something we just had to get through."

In my heart I added, "And so will you," to his sentence. Convinced Jim understood, I felt free to share my real thoughts with him now. "If I had only known it was coming," I said starting to cry, "I could have been more prepared."

"I had a close friend," Jim continued, "who died at forty-five. His cancer was so bad he lost down to where he was just skin and bones, and then he lay in bed for months suffering. You wouldn't have wanted that for Tom."

Even though I could not stop the tears, I found hope in Jim's story today. He hadn't gotten over losing his dad, but he had gotten *through* it. Maybe I would too. Now when I answer Jim's calls and hear him ask, "How are you doing?" I'll know he really wants to know.

∂∾∾

One year and four months before Tom died, I was hired by two partners in an architectural firm to be their secretary. In addition to being well respected architects, my bosses, Mike and Bruce, are also fine Christian men who begin each workday with prayer. I came back to work a week after losing Tom and I'm convinced I could not have managed my job without their help, prayers, and patience.

Many times in the days and weeks following Tom's death, I revisited the phone conversation I'd had with Mike the night Tom died. While I could not recall the words of his prayer it was a reminder that I had not been left alone to face this long dark night.

The morning after Tom's death I was surprised when Mike and Bruce knocked on my door. They'd never been to my house before, yet both of them took off work to come and talk with me for a while, and to pray. It helped me to tell them the details of how it happened and sense their concern.

Bruce came back the next day around lunch time to bring my paycheck, along with another check for one-thousand dollars and a turkey dinner with all the trimmings. Bills don't stop coming just because someone dies, and I knew I needed to figure out what and how much was due. Their gift would be enough to manage until after the funeral when I could work things out. I was blown away by their support.

Both of them came the night we received friends for Tom and also to his funeral. They stood nearby at the graveside service so I could see them, offering me the only real help there is for a widow. They showed me I was not alone.

When I went back to work they did little things to help me. I noticed a softer, quieter tone in their voices on the phone and in casual conversation, as if they shared my sorrow. The first time the delivery truck came from the office supply store where Tom worked, Bruce stood by my desk. He thought it might be hard for me, and he was right. Seeing someone else making deliveries in the truck Tom used to drive made me cry.

Mike would say, "Get your pencil," when he had something for me to do. He knew my mind was so muddled I couldn't remember even simple instructions unless I wrote them down.

I tried not to break down at work but sometimes the pain overwhelmed me and I fell apart. One day I was crying and shaking, just feeling sick inside, and it worried Mike and Bruce. They prayed for me, and then Bruce called his counselor friend to come talk with me in their library.

I felt crazy and out of control, but in the midst of all of that Bruce said, "One day you will be able to help someone that nobody else can."

One day...

Sunday, December 21, 2003 – 27 days later

Another Sunday morning and I can't make myself go back to church. It's too hard without Tom there beside me. I feel empty and forsaken by God. I can't stop asking, "Why? Why did God want to hurt me? Why did He take Tom from me? When I begged Jesus for help in my frantic attempt to revive Tom that night, why didn't He come?" I feel betrayed. "Why wouldn't the God I love help me?"

Then I remembered Job, a man introduced in the Scriptures as perfect and upright, one who feared God and shunned evil. It seemed cruel that God allowed Satan to wound him so deeply. Why? Job's story fueled my anger, since Satan could only do to Job what God permitted. I never imagined I could come to a place where the Scriptures offer no comfort for me, and where preaching and hymns about a loving God are offensive, yet here I am. I can't pray now. What's the use? Whatever God wants will be and I can't change that. Twenty–five years a Christian and now I've lost my faith.

chapter **2**
My Darkest Christmas

Wednesday, December 24, 2003 – thirty days later, Christmas Eve

NO MATTER HOW hard the Grinch and I tried to stop it, Christmas is here. My first one without Tom. It's Christmas Eve and Tom should be here helping me organize our party before the kids come. We are supposed to be making all their favorite snacks and wrapping silly prizes for the "reindeer" games. Sometime today Tom needs to slip away and hide the special present he always gives me. He should be here, but every memory screams, "Never again!"

The idea of our traditional Christmas without Tom smothers me, and I know I cannot do it this year. At least Tom and I had finished our shopping before he died and bought the kids' gifts. Dread replaced my usual Christmas spirit until Debbie called to invite our whole family to have dinner at Santo's, the restaurant she and her husband own.

"Do you have plans for Christmas?" Debbie asked.

"No, not really," I said. "We're leaning toward Taco Bell, but nothing is definite."

"Why don't all of you come to Santo's on Christmas Eve?" she asked. "I'll be working."

"OK," I said, "that sounds much better than a taco."

Dining at Santo's is always a treat, but tonight it was a place to be sheltered from the pain. Debbie reserved a large round table for us near the piano, and Michael played all of our requests. When he played the theme song from *Titanic*, tears spilled out as I contemplated the words, "*In my dreams I see you, I feel you, and that is how I know you go on.*"

The evening was bittersweet—beautiful and awful. Beautiful because we were encircled by friends; awful because I sensed Tom so near. I was at peace, and yet I felt cheated because Tom was not there. I could not stop crying.

We sat for a while after dinner, just listening to the music and soaking up the love of our friends. When we stood up to leave Debbie came over to our table.

"After the holidays, why don't we get together one night a week for dinner or a movie?" she asked.

"That sounds good. It will give me something to look forward to," I said.

Tonight, Debbie gave us special gifts—the company of friends, a delicious meal, a flawless serenade, and one more that far surpassed the others. She gave us a sweet memory in the midst of woe and, even though sorrow had stolen my joy, I looked forward to a night out with her.

We sat in silence on the drive home. There was no laughter in the living room as John David passed out presents. We missed Tom. I reflected on the way Tom insisted we take turns opening gifts and holding them up for the others to see. He always kept one package for me hidden until after everyone had finished and started to clean up, and then he dragged it out to surprise me.

The night was somber. When the kids started to leave, loneliness engulfed me.

"Come home with us," Tammy said. "You can spend the night."

"I'll be OK," I said. "Besides, you have places to go tomorrow. I will just have to get used to this – it's what my life is now."

∾∾

A night out with Debbie each week was my oasis, even though I often blubbered over dinner. It is not easy to be with a widow in the early months of grief, but Debbie stuck with me through the rough patches. After dinner we sometimes saw a movie or browsed the bookstore. Over the next few months we shopped at Wal-Mart for birdfeeders, watched a production of *Jesus Christ Superstar*, and went to a Laundromat to wash sheets. One morning, I woke up dizzy and called Debbie at 4:30 a.m. She rushed over, drove me to the emergency room, sat with me through testing, and then picked up my prescriptions before driving me home.

To escape the grief I wrote non-stop and sent copies to Debbie. She kept them in her nightstand until the weight broke the drawer. Night after night I sat at the computer weeping as I typed emails to Debbie, and she responded to every one. She didn't use religious clichés, e, or tell me to get over it. She merely tried to understand.

"I don't have all the answers," Debbie said, "but I do know God is real and He loves us." When my tears made it difficult to see the screen, Debbie wrote, "I'm crying too." These three words helped me most of all.

Amid a barrage of "whys", Debbie's simple truth tugged at my heart and held my faith intact. She was right. No matter what, Jesus loves me.

Thursday, December 25, 2003 – 31 days later, Christmas Day

    Something's Gotta Give opened today at Reel Theaters. For weeks Tom and I had watched the previews on television anticipating our date for the matinee on Christmas Day. Can it be possible Tom was here with me just a few weeks ago making holiday plans? It feels like a lifetime ago. I decided to keep our date and for the first time went to the movies alone.

    "One ticket for *Something's Gotta Give*," I said.

    Tom would have stopped at the concession stand for popcorn with extra butter, but I went straight into the theater. With ten minutes to go until starting time plenty of seats were open, so I slipped into a spot in the back against the wall away from the others.

    Couples dotted the theater as the lights dimmed and previews of coming attractions flashed across the screen. In the dark I almost felt Tom beside me and my heart ached for it to be true. Tom was supposed to be there – we had marked it on the calendar. How can I finish our life without him?

    After the movie I hurried to the car feeling emptier than I ever had before. Tears blurred my vision as I drove away.

    "I am alone," I said to myself, "so alone."

    Minutes crawled by all afternoon and I searched for a distraction to take my mind off Tom's absence and give me a break from the misery. I plopped down into the recliner, turned on the television, and flipped through channels. Nothing worked; the hole was too deep. At times like this

I used to talk to Jesus about the problem or write a letter to Him if I felt overwhelmed, but not since Tom died.

I begged Jesus for help that night but He let Tom die. I felt abandoned. My head tells me the Lord is still here, just as He has always been, but my heart says, "He hurt you; don't trust Him." I am the drowning man who won't take the hand of his rescuer.

I can't see any light now and my faith is working against me, because I believe God is omnipotent with total control over our lives. He could have given us more time. God knew our plans and the way our lives were meshed together. He knew where I would be without Tom. He knows whether I will pass this test or give up. He knows. How can I ask for God's help when He brought me to this place? Wounded and desperate I sat down at the computer and began to write...

"Dear God,

It's been a long time since we talked. I know you see my heart now so I won't pretend to be fine. Don't You think people spend too much time pretending things are fine when they know they're not?

Until one month ago I believed You loved me and walked close by my side wherever I went, I felt Your presence. So why did You leave me when I needed You most? And why did You take Tom away from me? People are afraid to ask You why. They think, like the character from Joan of Arcadia, they will burst into flames. It's funny how people think only what they say matters when You know their hearts. I just want to be real, and even if I fail and miss Heaven I don't want to still be pretending things are fine.

I'm angry with You and wonder why You want to hurt me. I thought I could run to You and hide when life turned so black I couldn't see, but You wouldn't help me that night. You took Tom away. I don't understand. Is it Your will for me to suffer all my life? Did I do something so severe that You want to punish me forever? Tom and I were a team and without him I am not a complete person. You told us to become one and then You ripped him out of my life. Help me understand.

What now? What will my fate be, a lifetime of loneliness or poverty? Will I be sick or crippled? Will I die suddenly or linger as a burden to my family and friends? You know me, whether or not I will surrender. Right now I feel weak and giving up would be easy, but I know Christy needs me. You gave me dreams after the death of my grandparents to help me have peace. Will You at least do that for me now so I can see Tom happy in Heaven and soothe my aching heart?

You are God and I am nothing, so why would You bother with me? The newspaper is full of deaths every day and Tom's was just one more. I am a speck of dust in the desert and You have no reason to explain or comfort me but I hope You will answer anyway.

Cathy"

There, I did it. I finally stopped shunning God and told Him how I felt. It wasn't the kind of prayer I used to write, and it felt bad to be angry with the God I loved, but it was honest. What now? Would God burn me to a cinder for daring to be so gruff with Him or would He love me anyhow? Whatever the outcome, it was my true worship for I came seeking Him with my whole heart.

❧❧

In time I began to communicate more with the Lord and gradually the letters became less angry. After a few months I began to end my written prayers with *"Thanks"*, *"Sincerely"*, or *"Love"* rather than just my name, and then on September 19, 2004 I wrote, *"I love You, Cathy."* In these letters I expressed my real thoughts to the Lord regardless of how terrible they were. I wrote as if speaking to someone in the room, and for sure I was...

February 18, 2004:

Dear Lord,

> *Are You still here? I can't see You, I can't feel You. You promised never to leave me or forsake me, but I feel alone and forsaken now. I don't think I can live without Tom. I know it is selfish of me to want him back when he is happy in Heaven, but I miss him so terribly. Why couldn't he stay a little longer?*
> *I'm empty now and the lessons I have taught others about the Scriptures and You don't even bring me comfort. People say those things to me now and my heart can't receive it. I am a well that won't hold water. I've talked a good talk but now I see how weak I am. I'm not afraid of dying; I'm afraid of living. Life is too empty without Tom.*
> *I shouldn't grieve because Tom is with You and he wouldn't come back even if he could, even if he knew my heart was broken. I know we all have to die and death is only a separation, yet I mourn because Tom is gone and my life has crumbled. Will You help me again? Will you have mercy again? Will You give me peace? I just need to find hope again.*
> *I should be thankful for all the people who love me and try so hard to do or say something that will make a differ-*

*ence. I find myself wanting to be better for them, yet the
darkness never ends. What does Your will plan for me?
Does the loneliness ever stop?*

Cathy

March 23, 2004:

Dear God,

    *Today I can't bear the loneliness and emptiness of being
without Tom. You gave us a special love and then You
took him away. Why? I am surrounded by people who
care about me and want to help, but I still feel alone. You
see my heart, the anger, resentment, and bitterness – all
things unbecoming a Christian. Have I been living a
lie all along and this is just Your way of showing me?
Perhaps after all this time I've only fooled myself and in
reality served You just for the loaves and fishes. I feel as
though I'm failing as a Christian and the guilt of my anger toward You bears on me. I could act as if nothing was
wrong, since I know how to look good to the world after
twenty-five years of worship. I could be in Church today
singing familiar songs, going through the motions, and
pretending I was fine, and nobody would know what's
really happening in my heart except You. But then who
else's opinion matters? One of the first prayers I remember
was, "Lord help me be real. I don't want to spend my life
in church then be lost in the end." So, I'll go on being real.
Please give me some answers to the questions that torment
me. Why did You take Tom away with no warning?
Why did You leave me here? Will You take me now? I
don't want to be here without Tom. You said we should
be one flesh and we were, then Tom died and my flesh
was torn in two. Why? Why couldn't we have more time?
Did I do some terrible thing I'm being punished for? You*

promised to always be with me, yet I feel abandoned. Where are You?

Through the years You warned me about other deaths, yet when the love of my life died You were silent. Tom was ripped from my life in an instant and now I'm closer to death than to life. I don't understand why You didn't come that night or why You wouldn't help me when Tom was dying. It felt like You were standing there with arms crossed watching while Tom was dying in my arms. Why? I was helpless, but You weren't. You could have given us more time. Why didn't You at least let us say goodbye? Will You answer any of these questions?

I can't carry this weight anymore. People tell me You have a plan for me, but wasn't Your plan for Tom and me together? Is Your plan for me to ache so deeply I dread waking in the morning? Before Tom died, every night I lay on my pillow and held You in my heart assured I was safe in Your hands. Now I find myself lying down and wondering if I will wake in the morning or if tomorrow will bring more tragedy. I'm afraid to go forward and I don't know how. I don't even know who I am without Tom. You have the power to heal my heart and give me peace. Will You? Have You forgotten me? Life has become unbearable. Please deliver me or let me die with Tom.

Cathy

May 3, 2004:

Lord,

If You are looking into my heart today You see the darkness. What is to become of me now? Did I do some awful thing You want me to suffer for? What about forgiveness? What about unconditional love? What about a Heavenly Father who would gather me under His wing?

Must life always be so difficult? So many questions – will You answer? Before Tom died I felt safe in You and found refuge when life was too hard, but since then I have felt alone. You promised never to let go of my hand, but where are You? I confess the hardness of my heart against the Church and You. I find myself wondering why I tried and if everything Tom and I did was in vain.

You see my angry heart and my broken spirit. You know my beginning and You know my end. I can't bear this grief and I can't change my heart. You have control but I can't reach You anymore. Like David, I leave my fate in Your hands. Will You have mercy or judgment? Will You heal me or let me die? If Your love for me is uncon-ditional, will You help me know it? Today, You are the father I thought loved me but when I was alone and frightened You stood back and watched from a distance. I trusted You to love and protect me and believed You would always be there, "Even to the end of the world." What happened?

You know how much I depended on Tom's love, and without him I am not complete. I have given up and lost hope. I have no plans or goals, no expectations of what lies ahead or of work I could do for You. All these years I've searched for people to influence for You, and asked for guidance to reach them, some small act that might make a difference. Now I feel lost and people are trying to reach me. Is that Your plan, to show me how fragile I really am?

Tom and I were small and insignificant in Your world but until he died I believed we were special to You. Now I see I am nothing. I looked at You as my friend, confi-dant, and protector, but now I see You as the all powerful God. The message of the potter and the clay is clearer— You are the potter who made the world and everything in it and You control what will be. My life is the broken pot, empty and worthless. What will happen now? Will I be discarded as damaged goods because I can't overcome the hurt and keep walking?

Cathy

June 20, 2004:

Dear Lord,

It's been seven months and I still don't want to live. What is to become of me? Will I be alone for 20 years? Will I become bitter or move on? Will I feel Your love again and find the safe haven I once knew? I feel far from You, as if I am such a disappointment You are punishing me. Did I love Tom too much? Did we neglect to pray enough, study, or do what You wanted? Are You looking at me now saying, "What a pity, I hoped you would do better"?

I am sure You will want to use my suffering to help others, but I don't want to reach out. I don't want to move or talk or live. I just want to be with Tom. I am with Tom – his heart and mine are one, yet I still breathe. Why? The song says, "All I had to offer Him was brokenness and strife," and that is what is left in me. I am hurt and angry and lonely, still trying to understand why You didn't help Tom and me.

Cathy

July 27, 2004:

Dear Jesus,

Do You love me? Will You come to me again? Speak to me? Deliver me from this deep hole of sadness? I miss Tom. My life is empty and I am becoming cold and bitter. Is that my fate now? You used to come in my sleep and speak to me and give me answers to deep problems. Why won't You come? Have I failed You or drifted so far away I can't hear You anymore? Life is full of pain, so much pain I can't bear it. You promised not to put more on us than we are able to bear but, Lord, I can't bear this.

I am so tired, body and soul that I don't want to keep searching or trying. Last night I felt so weak I imagined You might come for me soon. Will You? Life is a burden with long hard empty days and even longer nights. Does Tom still know about me? That I exist? That I love him? Will You give him my love?

I know You have placed people in my life to help me go forward, but I don't want to. I see my friends happy with their husbands having dinner parties and planning vacations and resentment creeps in knowing I can't. Retired couples remind me the plans Tom and I made will never be. I know Tom is with You, free and happy, and I thank You for not allowing him to suffer and for enabling him to do all the things he wanted until the second he died. I am just lost here on my own. How can I move through life without Tom?

"Ask and you shall receive," You said.

I ask You to deliver me from this loneliness and bring peace to my soul. You have given me three dreams of Tom to help me cope. Will You send another? I can't bear this loss, I can't. Tom was my love, my life.

Sincerely,

Cathy

August 17, 2004:

Dear Lord,

I know You want me to heal and move forward and I believe You love me. I don't want to feel angry and isolated, yet how do I find my way back? You gave Tom and me a special bond and made us one. How do I cope with losing him? I still want to follow him into death. What is my reason for living? How can I be whole again? Where do I belong? I feel so lost now, but I want to be reunited with Tom in Heaven so please show me the way back.

I know Tom is young, happy, and healthy with You and his life goes on. I know You want me to make it, and although I don't understand, I accept the bigger picture only You can see and that there is a reason for Tom's death. I know there are no answers to the questions a widow asks about losing her husband. I know we all have to die and I guess I knew Tom would be first, I just didn't expect it to be so soon. We had twenty-five years together, but even if You had given us ten or twenty more I am convinced I wouldn't have been ready to lose him.

I miss having someone to love me, someone to think I'm special and care about the little things in my life. My friends want me to be better and, while they try to stay in touch, they also have a real life I don't fit into. I don't want to be an albatross around their necks, someone they dread to see coming, and I don't want to intrude in their lives. I want my own life back.

I don't think I can make it without Tom. Everything I am, everything I do, and every place I go reminds me of him and the life we built. I don't want to start over and I don't want to take any more steps. What's next? What is to become of me? Will life just grind me up? I am sad, lower than I've ever been, and weary of my days. I suppose I have come to the place where Elijah was when he sat under the juniper tree in deep depression. Unlike

Elijah, I don't think I am the only one left serving You. Quite the contrary, I think You have servants all around eager to carry out Your will. You don't need me, You never did. I don't want to be lost, but I don't want to go back to Church either. I know I can't quit and just go inside my house, lock the door, and wait for time to pass. Will You show me some light, some truth, something real for my life?

With my will I want to love and praise You because I remember Calvary and I have known Your love, even though I can't feel it today. You said You are the same yesterday, today, and forever, so if You loved me before Tom died You still do. I believe, Lord, help my unbelief.

Love,

Cathy

September 19, 2004:

Dear Lord,

Thank You for the dream and letting me hold Tom. Thank You for the reminder from Rev. Hill that You gave Tom to me.

I am sorry for the anger. Help me to trust You, Lord. I am too weak to stand or walk, will You hold me? Will You help me know the truth about Heaven? Will Tom and I have the same personality there, know the things we know here, do the things we love? Is he there loving me still and asking You to help me? When I think of the rich man who lifted up his eyes in Hell and begged for help for his family I wonder if Toms asks You to take care of us. There are so many mysteries I can't comprehend, but I know Tom is with You at this moment.

You gave Tom a life of 60 years with health and happiness here before You called him home. As I watched the

*movie about a young man who was undergoing chemo-
therapy for leukemia I suddenly became very glad You
didn't allow Tom to suffer. When I saw the terrible sick-
ness and pain this young man endured I knew I couldn't
have watched Tom hurting like that. I would rather have
died myself. So with all the faith and love and trust I can
muster I praise You that Tom simply stopped breathing
and went to Heaven.*

*Where do I belong, Lord? Is there a place where I can be
just who I am in You? Help me find my way. Would You
tell Tom I love him and that I grew some yellow roses in
the backyard for him?*

I Love You,

Cathy

November 10, 2004:

Dear Jesus,

*You say, "I know the plans I have for you, plans not to
hurt you but to give you hope and a future."*

*What do You have planned for me, Lord? Where do I be-
long? What is my real life? It feels as if I've been caught in
a tornado and am waiting to be dropped into what will
become my life. Will I be able to manage the house? The
yard? The car? Will I be sick? Old and feeble? Will I always be alone? Is writing part of my future?*

*I feel so lost and sick at heart missing Tom to hold me.
You know how much I love Tom and how our hearts are
joined. How can I go on without him in my life? Help
me understand what is happening and where my life that
seems to be spiraling out of control is going. You said You
would be near to those with a broken heart. Are You
near? Are You with me, Lord? I'm afraid, just afraid.*

I know You love me, I feel it, but I still don't want to study, attend church, or listen to preachers. What's wrong with me? I have come to a strange place, a place where death means being with Tom and life is to be endured. Will You help me find the desire to live and the strength to keep going? This morning on my way to work I looked ahead into the smoky purple haze on the mountain and wished I could drive into it and never come back. What will change that? I am not angry anymore, and I'm glad Tom gets to be in Heaven. I just don't want to stay here without him.

I give up, Lord. I thought I was a strong Christian when Tom and I tried to follow You, but without him I can't move, Please help me not to discourage others with my actions, and if Tom and I helped anyone before don't let me tear it down now.

With Love,
Cathy

In grief counseling I learned wounded emotions are slow to heal and you can't trust feelings. This poem is a reminder that you must make decisions according to what you know to be true and let your actions be guided by the will. The sailboat paperweight on my desk at work gives me confidence I am not alone on the journey. Engraved on its sail are these words, "The will of God will never lead you where the grace of God cannot keep you."

WILL

By: Ella Wheeler Wilcox

One ship drives east, and another west

With the self-same winds that blow;
'Tis the set of the sails
And not the gales,
Which decides the way to go.

Like the winds of the sea are the ways of fate;
As the voyage along through life'
'Tis the will of the soul
That decides its goal,
And not the calm or the strife.

Even when I tried to push God away in anger He was always near, and instead of judging me He sent people to love and help me. All the while I was mad at God I expected His judgment for my negative attitude toward Him. I expected it, believed it would come, and didn't care. It didn't matter how terrible a penalty He imposed on me as long as He let me die when it was over. I didn't try to please God and I didn't want to hear anything about Him. I told myself I didn't matter to Him after all, and for the next year every time Jesus tried to love me I rejected Him. When I wouldn't let Him comfort me, He sent others to love me and I knew it. Still, I didn't respond. I didn't want His help. I didn't want to need Him anymore after he abandoned me that night.

The Lord didn't give up on me, but kept reaching out with His love until I could no longer resist. He loved me whether I was doing things to please Him or lashing out in anger. He didn't stop loving me when I pushed Him away. When I finally responded to His love it was as if nothing had ever happened. He had been with me all the time and nothing I said or did changed His love for me. In my storm I found true unconditional love. God was not a harsh taskmaster waiting for me to stumble so He could burn me to a cinder, but rather my Heavenly Father wooing me back to Him. He wanted me to be healed and whole and make it to Heaven. That is why Jesus went to Calvary.

It took a year for me to return to church and even longer to find my way back into life and the faith I had known.

On December 21, 2004 I wrote:

Lord,

> *I resisted Your provision because I was mad at You. Although I recognized Your intervention when people came to help me, rather than thanking You I said, "You don't have to help me, I'm not going to do anything for You." How could I have been so arrogant, knowing that except You give me breath I could not even have those thoughts? Still, You didn't leave me. If I listed all those who came to support me it would be difficult to explain how I stayed angry with You for almost a year. You never stopped reaching for me with Your love, even when I closed my heart.*

> *I didn't want to trust You again and I told myself if You really loved me You wouldn't have hurt me. You knew I would react the way I did when Tom died and You loved me through it. I still don't understand why he died so soon, but in Your eyes death of the righteous is a beautiful thing, the doorway to eternal life with You.*

> *Thank You for giving me Tom for twenty-five happy years and for staying close to me after he left. You loved me even when I was mad at You, so mad I wouldn't acknowledge Your presence. I was crazy to keep going under when I could just have taken Your hand.*

I love you.
Cathy

❧❧

Church without Tom is unbearable. It had been the center of our lives for twenty-five years and the place where Tom and I were a team. The first time I walked through the church doors without Tom the weight of his absence fell on me and I could hardly breathe. Walking to the pew, pain gave way to anger as my focus turned toward God and the haunting question that burned within me, "Why?"

I soon realized it is impossible to worship and sing praises to someone you are mad at, even when that One is God. I left the Church for almost a year, during which I neither tithed nor read the Bible, and my only prayer was to ask why. "Why did You take Tom? Why have You forsaken me? Why? Why? Why?" I ranted at God and then braced myself for His judgment to fall.

Instead of reciprocating with wrath, Jesus came closer. I felt Him reach for me, trying to hold me – to love me, but I wouldn't let Him. Unscathed by my rejection Jesus kept reaching, and when I refused His embrace He sent others in His stead.

chapter 3
A New Year Without Tom

THURSDAY, JANUARY 1, 2004 – 39 days later, New Year's Day

Every New Year's Day I take inventory of my life, evaluate areas I need to change, and tell myself, "Hey, this is a brand new year; you can start over again." In assessing relationships in my life I think of ways to be closer. When I was a young, over-zealous Christian I tried to figure out how to reach people for the Lord. I believed like the characters on the television show, *Touched by an Angel*, that one small act could change a life completely. What a dreamer I was, an eccentric if truth be told. This is the real world, and today all I can think about is the anguish of facing next year without Tom.

At 10:00 a.m. the phone rang. It was Jenny.

"Come over for lunch today," Jenny said. "We're having black-eyed peas and hog jowl."

"I appreciate the offer," I said, "but I can't."

"Come on over," Jenny pleaded. "You can just eat lunch and leave. It'll be good for you."

I declined Jenny's invitation but she would not take no for an answer. She kept calling back every twenty minutes until I agreed to come for lunch. The sorrow was winning today, and all I wanted to do was curl up in a ball and forget about life. New Year's Day points to the future, the thing I couldn't bear to think about knowing Tom would not be there.

I knew Jenny would not give up, so I got dressed and went for lunch. I was miserable, and making conversation required more strength than I could muster. I was such poor company I left soon after we ate. Still, I was glad I went, because sitting home alone on a holiday fuels depression. At times of deep sadness I don't want to move, but I have to go on and sometimes I need a friend to love me enough to keep pushing until I do.

❧ ❧

Jenny is not only my friend but also my cousin. In the months before Tom died we had become closer friends with Jenny and her husband Larry. In June the four of us had spent a day together at Roane Mountain to view the rhododendrons at their peak.

Jenny and I were together on Sunday, the day before Tom died, and I remember telling her how lost I would be without him. Tom and I always spent Sunday afternoons together, but he had wanted to stay home that day and do some finishing touches on the sunroom. When I went to the mall with Jenny, I had no inkling it was to be my last Sunday with Tom. I rarely buy clothes for Tom unless he is with me, but he needed khaki dress pants and Penney's had them on sale so I made an exception. Besides, I could always return them if they didn't fit. Tom never got a chance to try the pants on because he died the next day. Jenny took care of my return.

Jenny made sure I didn't hibernate in isolation, and called when she didn't hear from me for a few days. One Saturday, Jenny and Larry asked me to go to North Carolina with them for a landscape show, and Jenny insisted on buying a flower for me to plant to remember our day. It was the first one I ever planted, and it lived.

If I had an awful day and called Jenny, she insisted I come over, and most of the time she cooked supper for me. When I was ready to leave, Jenny packed leftovers for me to take home, and once she even sent a cup of her homemade pimento cheese with me to pack in my lunch.

Most Fridays Jenny and Larry can be found at Cracker Barrel after work, and they often invite me to meet them there. One day while I was driving home from Pigeon Forge, trying to decide where to stop for a burger, my cell phone rang. It was Jenny calling to say she was cooking supper if I would like to come over. After dining alone so much, having someone to share a meal with is as nice as eating it. After supper Larry made a pot of coffee and we retired to the living room to chat.

I clocked many hours crying on their couch in my first year of working through grief, and oftentimes I drove home after dark.

"Call me when you get in," Jenny said, "so I know you are safe."

Their love and concern was my shelter.

Saturday, January 10, 2004—47 days later

Today at one p.m. I met with Reverend Arne Walker, our Pastor for the past three years. I didn't know what to expect. Would he join the others that tried to help by quoting scriptures or throwing religious clichés my way? I hoped not.

"You have to walk through grief," Pastor began, "and it's good to have people who love you to walk through it with you."

I was surprised and relieved as Pastor Walker continued with his insight about grief. He talked of troubled youths he had counseled and found that a large percentage of the ones hooked on drugs and alcohol had experienced some big loss and didn't work through the grief.

"Someone told them they needed to be strong," he said, "so they repressed the pain with substances that only masked it."

"I'm not trying to be strong," I said. "When people ask how I'm doing I tell them crummy."

"I worry more about the people who lose someone and seem to be fine," he said, "than people like you."

When I told him I fall apart at times he said, "I don't like that term. It's a normal part of grief, but people are often uncomfortable with the tears and want to try to help you stop. There is no right or wrong way to grieve, and no set time."

Pastor Walker gave me a book, *Don't Take My Grief Away From Me,* by Doug Manning, but my lack of concentration makes it hard to focus enough to read. His words and presence comforted me, and before he left Pastor Walker asked me to come back to church.

"Church will be my biggest obstacle," I said, "because Tom and I were a team there. Besides, I haven't gotten past the anger with God for taking him."

Pastor quickly challenged my remark, "I am not happy with the idea that 'God took Tom'," he said. "We are just victims of the genes our parents gave us."

After Pastor Walker left I went to visit my Aunt Velma and we talked for over an hour. When I got back home there were four messages on my answering machine from people who, as Pastor said, "Are walking through grief with me." This was a good day.

కావ

I didn't return to Church as Pastor Walker asked, but he continued to minister to me by sending Church bulletins, handwritten highlights from his sermons, poems, personal notes, and even postcards from vacations in places like Bozeman, Montana and Mexico. He wrote, "You are loved and prayed for and missed," and, "you are a part of our Church family and have been knit together by Christ." I kept every one.

Several months later on a Wednesday night, I went to the Church for the baptism of Kathy's three grandchildren. When Pastor Walker saw me walk in he told me how happy he was to see me there. After the service, I met him in the hallway on my way out and paused for a moment to speak to him.

"How are you?" he asked.

"OK," I said. "That's as good as it gets without Tom."

"I feel as if I've failed because I wasn't able to help you," Pastor Walker said.

More important than his words was the concern I saw on his face. He cared about me and wanted me to be healed and restored, and for those struggling through grief the greatest help comes from knowing someone is there. It had been a year since I stopped coming to Church, yet Pastor Walker had not allowed my rejection to push him away. He was with me, and that made all the difference.

I didn't tell Pastor Walker how much he helped me that night, but I came back to Church the next week and asked him to be my Spiritual Director. We began meeting for half an hour on Wednesdays and Pastor Walker helped me work through the grief. He motivated me to write, and encouraged me to look for what God was up to in my life. He left this poem with me for inspiration:

Before You Can Dry Another's Tears – You Too Must Weep!
By: Helen Steiner Rice

Let me not live a life that's free
From "the things" that draw me close to Thee
For how can I ever hope to heal
The wounds of others I do not feel
If my eyes are dry and I never weep,
How do I know when the hurt is deep
If my heart is cold and it never bleeds,
How can I tell what my brother needs

For when ears are deaf to the beggar's plea
And we close our eyes and refuse to see,
And we steel our hearts and harden our mind,
And we count it a weakness whenever we're kind,
We are no longer following the Father's way
Or seeking His guidance from day to day
For, without "crosses to carry" and "burdens to bear,"
We dance through a life that is frothy and fair,
And "chasing the rainbow" we have no desire
From "roads that are rough" and "realms that are higher"
So spare me no heartache or sorrow, dear Lord,
For the heart that is hurt reaps the richest reward,
And God enters the heart that is broken with sorrow
As He opens the door to a brighter tomorrow,
For only through tears can we recognize
The suffering that lies in another's eyes.

Monday, January 26, 2004—Two months later

The sorrow was crushing me as I stood in the doorway of our big walk-in closet. Tom was there in his clothes, his shoes, his smell. I could not go in. Two months have passed and still everything in our bedroom is just as Tom left it—his watch and glasses on the nightstand, his toothbrush in the holder next to mine, his razor in the cabinet drawer. Fragments of his daily routine are vehicles of unimaginable pain for me.

"Tom is gone," I said out loud, "and he is not coming back."

I told myself I needed to stop trying to hold onto Tom, pretending he'd just gone away for awhile. Keeping his clothes seemed to make the pain even more unbearable. It was time to face reality. I decided to take Tom's things out of the closet and box them up, but as I stepped through the doorway I had no way of knowing this would be the darkest night of my life.

I started to dismantle Tom's section in the closet and the weight on my heart became heavier with every shirt I took off its hanger, until I could hardly breathe. Alone! So alone! The night closed in around me, fear tightened its grip, and I lost hope. I just wanted the pain to end. Then I remembered the 22-caliber pistol Tom kept loaded in the nightstand beside our bed.

"It would only take a second," echoed in my head as I thought of the weapon. "It would only take a second, and then it would all be over."

How could I feel this way? How could I have thoughts of suicide? I was a Christian, wasn't I? It seemed so once, before this nightmare began. Now God feels a million miles away. Tom and I had been faithful Christians for twenty-five years and now Scripture, hymns, and preaching all seemed so hollow. I don't want to hear it. Where was God when Tom was dying in front of me? Why didn't He answer my screams for help? I felt hopeless, lost, abandoned. Where was the God of Abraham? Where was my God?

A battle raged within me. I wanted only to stop breathing and go to Heaven with Tom, but how could I? Would God let me into His Kingdom when I couldn't bear to sit in His church? Could I deliberately break His commandment, Thou Shalt Not Kill, and expect to enter glory? I was consumed by an unutterable sadness having lost the love of my life, and I was angry, angry with God for taking Tom, angry with myself for being so weak. With those feelings came overpowering guilt as I believed I was failing as a Christian. Where was my faith? I knew God's truth, but my emotions held me hostage.

I pushed back the dark imaginings and resumed sorting Tom's belongings, separating the things I wanted to keep. Every article was so unique, so Tom. Two identical pairs of Reebok high-top basketball shoes, his trademark, sat on the floor. How long had we searched in store after store for that exact style of shoe? It was the only one that fit him just right. Next, there were his old western boots with heels slightly higher than his other shoes, the ones he wore so he could be taller than me when I wanted to wear high heels, since we were both five feet nine inches tall.

Tom's clothes were divided into three sections, one for good, one for work, and one for tinkering around the house. "Good" meant church on Sunday, vacation, or going places for fun, and when they began to show wear they moved to the "work" section. These were to wear to work until they were too frayed, stained, or holes had worn in the back jean pockets revealing his underwear. Then they moved to the "tinkering" section for working around the house.

"Those are a little too sexy for work," I'd say. "You don't want to be flashing the women."

"They're just getting comfortable," he'd tell me, "and you want me to get rid of them."

It took some coaxing before Tom would concede to move them to his "tinkering" section because it meant he would have to buy more clothes, a chore he hated.

"Just a waste of money!" I can still hear him groan, "I'd rather buy a tool."

How could I pack all of those memories away? If I took away his clothes I'd have to admit he was never coming back. How could I? I thought of the pistol again.

I kept digging and sorting until I had emptied the closet of all Tom's clothes, then I could see boxes on the floor against the wall with treasures Tom had saved. Stacks of *Home Improvement* and *Woodworking* magazines reminded me of all the projects he planned that would now go unfinished. Next to the boxes was the huge glass bottle he had tossed coins into forever. I reminisced about the way Tom saved in little ways, pennies in a jar and larger coins in his cash register bank that calculated each addition and would not open until the total reached ten dollars. He stashed dollar bills in the top drawer of the hutch, and a few twenties in his old wallet in the nightstand. Almost every time I rearranged a drawer or closet after he died, I found a few dollars. I felt close to Tom when I found those little surprises, as if he were still taking care of me.

Sitting on the closet floor, I felt as empty as the clothes rack I was staring at. It was finished. I had taken Tom out of the room, just as his untimely death had taken him out of my life. It was late. I should get up and get ready for bed. But why? Why bother going through the motions of life anymore? Every day was twenty-four hours to be endured, not lived, and without Tom I felt dead already.

My mind wandered amidst the shadowy thoughts of death to an earlier time, before I met Tom, when I'd felt the same dark emotions. My first husband had left me for another woman after five years of marriage and I felt like an old shoe someone had thrown out. Standing in the restroom of the store where I worked, I held the razor blade I pulled out of my box cutter. I began to walk through the act in my mind imagining the way things would be after I was gone. Who would find me? Who would care? Nothing really mattered until I thought about my two-year-old baby, Christy. Who would pick her up from the babysitter? Who would raise her? Who would love her? Only two possibilities came to my mind: her father, who had abandoned her in our divorce, or my parents, emotionally crippled from problems of their own. I put down the blade and started to cry. Regardless of what happened in my life I loved my baby beyond measure, too much to condemn her to a life of anything less.

My thoughts went back to my childhood and to a girl not much older than me named Susie whose life was altered by her father's suicide. I met Susie when she came to visit her cousin, my friend Barbra who lived next door. Susie was an only child, adored by her parents, who had everything a kid could want. I envied her life, until her mother was diagnosed with aggressive breast cancer and then died within a few months. Susie's father, unable to cope with the grief, took his own life a short time later. Afterwards, Susie was different. The happy-go-lucky, spoiled child now seemed much older than her years with a deep sadness I could not take in.

I couldn't leave that legacy for my daughter. I stood up, turned off the closet light, and closed the door.

Struggling to shake the morbid thoughts, I told myself, "If you had used the razor blade in the restroom that day you never would have met Tom. You wouldn't have known twenty-five years of perfect love."

Tonight, things seem dark and hopeless, but what about tomorrow? I remembered a quote from *One Minute After You Die* by Erwin Lutzer, "Suicide is a permanent solution to a temporary problem."[1]

As I lay in our bed the nearby pistol still haunted my mind. It made me afraid, afraid of weak moments and of losing control. Before I finally fell asleep I promised myself if the dark thoughts had not lifted by morning I would call someone for help.

Morning came and the shadows remained. Reaching for the alarm I remembered the gun and knew I needed help. But who could I call? I didn't want to be locked up in a padded room. I dressed for work and told myself if the thoughts were still there when I got off, I would call Debbie.

I left the office at four-thirty and driving home I realized nothing had changed, thoughts of dying still occupied my mind. Before leaving home this morning I was resigned to confide in Debbie, but now I was reluctant to burden my friend with such a weight. If she knew, surely she would feel compelled to help me and how could I ask so much? Too weak to fight it alone, I had to reach out. I pulled into the carport, unlocked the door, and walked straight to the phone to make the call. Then, I saw the answering machine blinking—it was a message from Debbie.

"I just thought you might want to come over," Debbie said. "I'm home tonight and not doing anything. Give me a call."

Through tears I whispered, "Thank you," to the God I knew was watching. Then I pressed redial on the caller ID.

"I'm so glad you called," I confided, "I'll be there in a few minutes." When I walked through Debbie's front door I felt safe.

"Come in and sit down," she said, "and I'll make us some tea." Then she paused for a second and looked at me, "How are you?" she asked.

"I can't live without Tom," I confessed sobbing like a frightened child.

"You have to," Debbie said and put her arms around me. "You don't have a choice." She held me for a minute, sensing I was wrestling with thoughts of suicide. "As long as one person cares about you," Debbie said, "you can't do that."

I knew she was right. Debbie made us some tea and sat with me while my tears conveyed the pain no words could express. Debbie seemed to understand my inner turmoil and I was relieved to have told her. I also realized I couldn't manage my grief alone anymore. Tomorrow I would call Tom's friend, Jerry, a Baptist minister who leads a grief share group at his church.

❧❧

Tom met Jerry several years ago when they both ended up in the same landscaping class, and their friendship began. After the class they got to know each other better when Tom delivered office supplies to the church where Jerry was Associate Pastor. Tom had great respect for Jerry and often stopped by his office to talk or seek his counsel. In 2000 Tom was worried about my lingering depression after the loss of my mother and he went to Jerry to ask about the Griefshare Group he led. Jerry gave Tom a video for me to watch about the stages of grief, and it helped me.

When thoughts of suicide kept coming back, I remembered the video and thought of Jerry. I had met Jerry only once when Tom and I ran into him at Kroger. I wasn't sure he would remember me, but in desperation I called the church. Jerry told me there was no Griefshare Group in session at that time, but he offered to let me take the tapes home to watch. I set a time a few days later to meet with him and pick up the tapes. I still recall our first conversation...

"Hello," I said shaking Jerry's hand, "I'm Cathy Wilhelm, Tom's wife."

"How are you doing?" he asked.

I paused for a moment searching for words to respond. "I can't die, so I have to live," I said. It was the first time I'd told someone how I really felt. Life had become a chore to complete, a drudgery.

Jerry gave me the first tape in a series to watch and offered to meet with me individually for a few weeks. I made an appointment for the next week and each following week I met briefly with Jerry and picked up the next video. The tapes featured people that had suffered loss, mainly through the death of a loved one. One man told of coming home each day and sitting in the dark after his wife died, because the light had gone out of his life. Another asked God how he was supposed to live with only one arm, one leg, half a heart, etc. because the other half of him was gone. I began to understand what grief is. I wasn't the only one that knew this unbearable pain, this long, dark tunnel with no end in sight. As I listened to their stories and shared the pain I began to feel hope, knowing others had been where I was and made it through.

Soon the weekly Griefshare Sessions began in the church parlor every Wednesday at six p.m. The first night we sat at a large round table facing each other and one by one told our name and story of loss. At the end of the hour seven strangers had formed a bond from the mutual pain we tried to express. While grief is as unique as a fingerprint and different for everyone, we were all in a dark place. We started a journey toward healing that night and drew strength from each other in the weeks and months that followed.

Grief is hard work. It's like fighting a terrible monster that rips a person into teeny pieces with no warning and it never grows tired of attacking. The pain in that room was beyond measure, and yet through our tears we found comfort. There in the midst of others who, like you, were facing the unthinkable you somehow find the courage to inch forward.

There is no magic formula to take away the pain and no quick fix. Every week we met together and, though we left exhausted from the intense emotions we shared, it helped to be with others who understood and cared. That round table was an sanctuary, a safe place to share the hurt, get angry, or cry without feeling uncomfortable.

Each week we listened to taped speakers, pastors, counselors, and others working through grief. The greatest comfort comes from ones who have been there and understand what grief is. We talked about the emotions of grief, shock, numbness, denial, anger, guilt, fear, disorganization, panic, isolation, loneliness, depression, and even thoughts of suicide. We found out grief is a process and not a state of being—a journey with a history. We learned to keep walking, keep trusting, and we celebrated each small victory. Through the words of Jeremiah 29: 11 we encouraged each other with every step..."For I know the plans I have for you, declares the Lord, plans to prosper you and not to harm you, plans to give you hope and a future".

Saturday, February 14, 2004 – 3 months later

Weekends are tough because Tom and I had them off together. Even more so today since it's Valentine's Day and my sweetheart can't be here.

If Tom were here today we would get up early, have a cup of coffee, and read the paper. Before going out to work in the yard, Tom would make a big breakfast for us. Saturday was his catch-up day and he liked to start early and not, as he often said, "Waste my day." Tom would take a break at two in the afternoon to eat lunch and watch Yankee Workshop, but he usually fell asleep before Norm was finished. We seldom made plans or went places on Saturday, but rather stayed here and enjoyed our home.

"Even when I'm working outside," Tom said, "I like knowing you're here."

I felt the same about him and that is what I miss most of all – the everyday goings-on in our ordinary weekend.

I was pulled back into the present when Mary, a widow from Church, called to invite me to lunch. She lost her husband two years ago and I'm sure this is a hard day for her too. Mary and I met at Cracker Barrel and she handed me a book of daily readings about grief that was written from the author's personal experience.

"I read it all the time," Mary said, "because I find so much comfort there."

My suspicious nature wondered if Mary had been sent by the Church Council to ask me to come back, and this lunch invitation was a tactic. I was still angry with God and didn't want to mislead Mary.

"I feel I should tell you that I won't be coming back to the Church," I said, "Tom was the Lutheran, not me."

"That's ok," Mary said. "The Lord will show you where to go."

Mary had not been sent with an agenda at all, she came to help a new widow. We talked about our life now, and there was no need for me to explain what I was going through. Mary knew. I felt her love and compassion as one wounded heart to another, and it lifted my loneliness for a day.

☙❧

Mary and I had more lunch dates, saw a few movies, and went shopping now and then. We cried together many times and also laughed once in a while. We became friends, and when our hearts hurt we called each other.

"This stinks," I said.

"I know it," Mary said. "I hate it, but we will get through it."

Friday, February 20, 2004 – 3 months later

I had lunch today at Cracker Barrel with Patsy, a young widow Jenny arranged for me to meet. Patsy's husband died a month before Tom under similar circumstances and Jenny had no doubt we could help each other. I told her to give Patsy my phone number and ask her to call if she wanted to talk. Earlier this week Patsy called to invite me to lunch.

I recognized Patsy right away from Jenny's description of her, a petite woman with shoulder-length, dark hair.

"Are you Patsy?" I asked.

"Yes, and you must be Cathy," Patsy said.

Even before we sat down to eat, an instant bond formed between us. It was a connection fused by our mutual nightmare and the invisible wounds we bore.

"I heard about what happened to your husband," I said. "My bosses were discussing the death of a fifty-two-year-old man they knew named Charles. They said he had a heart attack at home and his wife tried to rush him to the hospital, but he died on the way. I thought of what you must have gone through and it was the worst scenario I could imagine. I had no way of knowing I would be where you were in just four weeks."

"Did your husband have a heart attack too?" Patsy asked.

"Yes, I think so," I said. "Something happened with his heart but I didn't have an autopsy performed to know for sure."

We spent the next hour sharing the details of our husbands' deaths and reassuring each other. As we talked

I noticed Patsy's tears, like mine, were never far from the surface .

I didn't see Patsy again until a few months later when we met in the Church parlor for the first Griefshare session, but before the night ended a true friendship had begun.

When the sadness started to crush us, we called each other and talked for hours. At times when we could not bear to be alone another minute, we crashed on each other's couches with a bowl of popcorn. Sometimes we rented a movie, or took a walk – anything to ease the pain. Since we worked in the same vicinity we often had lunch together. On Tom's birthday Patsy was concerned about me being alone, so she met me for dinner and a movie.

Tom always took care of the yard, so when I needed to use his hedge clippers for the first time to trim honeysuckle by the driveway, I was stressed out.

"You can do it," Patsy said, "I will come over and help you."

And she did. Early Saturday morning Patsy pulled into my driveway ready to tackle the honeysuckle, and with the two of us the task didn't seem as daunting.

Patsy not only shares my misery, she wants to find a way to help me through it. She is a safe place to cry without explaining the tears, and to reveal the deep sorrow and fear that overtakes me. With Patsy just a phone call away I know I am not alone.

Patsy extends every goodbye with saying, "I love you, and don't forget you can call me anytime."

I know she means it.

Thursday, March 25, 2004 – 4 months later

Tonight Christy and I went to Walgreens and ran into the nurse that coached Tom for years on how to eat right and manage his diabetes. She taught him how to give himself insulin shots using an orange, and gave him her phone number in case he ever had a question. She was very knowledgeable and compassionate, since her son also had diabetes. We had known her for ten years and become more than just acquaintances, yet there I stood unable to remember her name. My mind is so disoriented now I can barely function, and even the simplest things take all of my effort. Finally, it came to me—Rhonda!

"Where's Tom tonight?" Rhonda asked, "home building something?"

My heart sank. "You don't know about Tom...," I said pausing for a moment. "He died just before Thanksgiving." We both cried as I told her the details.

"Diabetes damages the heart," Rhonda explained, sensing my desperate need for answers. "The arteries become narrow and weak."

"How could the doctors not know he might die?" I pressed, almost interrogating.

"I see it all the time," she answered. "Patients will be doing fine, and then they die. Something can happen suddenly, electrical impulses in the heart, rhythm, or a blood clot. A clot can form instantly and there isn't anything anyone can do."

Very few things have helped me deal with the grief, but tonight Rhonda's words through tears soothed my heart. She listened to all my questions and anxieties about

Tom's death and responded with sincere concern and medical experience.

"I'm glad you were there with Tom," Rhonda added. "Even though it was hard for you, it gave him comfort."

"Did he know I was there?" I asked with tears streaming down my face.

"I'm sure he did," she insisted. "From watching the vital signs of dying patients, they hear even when they can't respond."

"You know," I said trying to control the tears, "people think I should be better by now."

"You shouldn't expect anything from yourself for a year, maybe longer," Rhonda reminded me. "Half of your life has been torn away. People who haven't gone through it can't know what it's like to lose your husband or wife."

She gave me a hug and I walked away with her words safely tucked away in my memory to be recalled each time the dark clouds return.

ॐ ॐ

I was terrified beyond words the night Tom died, and after talking to Rhonda maybe Tom was too. I'm glad we were together.

Trying to make sense of what happened that night tormented my mind. My probe for answers was relentless. Why? What went wrong? What could I have done to save Tom? I searched the Internet, called doctors, relived the scene, and prayed. Nothing could change what happened, but learning more about diabetes, heart disease, and even dying seemed to help me absorb the loss and begin to cope.

Meeting Rhonda that evening turned out to be an important part of my healing. Since she knew Tom personally, as well as the mechanics of diabetes and heart disease, Rhonda's sympathy was coupled with concrete medical facts about Tom's condition. She edged open the door to my dismal world and a tiny stream of light came in.

Sunday, March 28, 2004—4 months later

I woke this morning to a feeling of dread—another Sunday alone. Weekends are wearisome, but Sundays surpass my limit of endurance. I sipped coffee and read the newspaper, while I braced for another long day without Tom. It's warm and sunny outside—Tom's favorite kind of day. I want to jump in the truck with him and ride out to the lake. I want to touch him, tell him about my day, and maybe try out a new recipe on him. The ache spread through the core of my being, and nothing brought relief. I called Brenda.

"Come on over," Brenda said, "I'm making biscuits and gravy."

Brenda is a wonderful cook, and it was an offer I could not refuse. "OK," I said pushing back tears. "I'll be there in a minute."

"Come in and sit at the table," Brenda said opening the door. "That way we can talk while I cook."

Peace settled over me and I did not want to leave Brenda's kitchen. I stayed all afternoon, until I could find the courage to go home and face my empty house.

"I hate to leave," I said, "but I better head home."

"Stay all night," Brenda said.

I knew she wasn't just being nice, her offer was sincere. Although tempting, I did not spend the night, but I did stay long enough for my storm to pass.

෨๛

Brenda has a gift for making folks feel at home and her kitchen became my Sunday sanctuary. One morning

I knocked on her door sobbing after taking flowers to Tom's grave. Brenda invited me in, handed me a bowl of fancy cherries, and poured me a glass of tea.

She made time for me whenever I needed her shoulder, and if she had plans she took me along. We cashed in free coupons at Food City, looked for herbs at a local nursery, browsed a bookstore, and delivered cakes. Brenda is a history buff, so we even scoped out area cemeteries.

Eleven months after Tom died Brenda's and Jerry's youngest son, Micah, was killed in a camping accident. Feeling the weight of their loss I drove to the house hoping to comfort them. Brenda saw me walking toward the door and met me on the sidewalk. We both burst into tears, then stood there holding each other and wailing. The moment exemplified the card Brenda gave me when I lost Tom. It read, "Understanding is the greatest gift you can give a friend."

Tuesday April 06, 2004 – 5 months later

Today, I can't cope with missing Tom. The pain is unbearable. I woke up this morning longing for him to hold me. I stared at his empty chair while I had my coffee and tried to read the paper. Surrounded by his things, it still seems like he should come walking down the hall any minute. I know people get through this, but *when does it start to get better? Does the pain ever end?*

Every little thing is a reminder of our life together, and after twenty-five years it is hard to be me without Tom. Songs trigger bittersweet memories, so I've stopped listening to the radio. Every night we watched *Wheel of Fortune* and *Jeopardy* and now they make me relive his death. Last Thursday, I hurried through the grocery store to get home by nine o'clock to watch *CSI,* and then a wave of sadness washed over me as I walked to the car. Those were our shows and now they are remnants of a life I can't have. I cried Saturday when I fed the birds and saw the flowers Tom planted coming up.

I can't even escape the memories at work. Sometimes when I answer the phone I think of times Tom called me there.

"Who is this?" Tom always said.

Tom was from the old school, a dedicated company person. He thought I should always introduce myself when answering a call.

"Everyone knows me except you," I'd tell him every single time. It was our little chuckle.

Tom has always been just a phone call away but now I can't reach him. I left Tom's message on our answering machine, and when I call home to hear his voice it seems real for a few seconds. I cling to every syllable and, even when I force myself to accept the awful truth, Tom's voice still comforts me.

❧ ❧

In the early months there seemed to be no relief, no peace. Tom and I planned our future together, our life in retirement, then in one minute it was swept away. Our life ended and my new life began—a transition that required me to step forward whether I wanted to or not.

At first I was afraid and convinced I could not manage alone but, one day at a time and one crisis at a time, I survived the first year...Then the second. I needed a new roof, and then the outside spigot started leaking. I found out you somehow find the strength to keep going and do what is necessary. Now, I don't panic so much when the toilet leaks or the gutter plugs up. I learned to take care of the yard, the house, and the car, and when something was beyond my ability I found someone more capable. I called friends and family or pestered my bosses for direction. Learning to lean on others was difficult because I did not want to be a burden. Now I'm learning to do things I never considered when I had Tom. I painted the kitchen, repaired wallpaper, caulked a tub, and even stained my deck—all things he would have handled.

I don't have Tom, but I'm not alone. When fear seizes my spirit, I go over scenarios of problems in my mind and then count all the people I could call for help. It is quite a long list and there is always someone who will come. Life has not worked out as we intended but I know God still has a plan for me. I still have a future and with His help and a little help from my friends I can make it on my own.

Good Friday, April 9, 2006 – 5 months later

Tonight I went to Church for the Good Friday Service of Darkness and I cried the entire time. Kathy started the service with a solo, *I Love You Written in Red,* and when she sang, "*I love you, I love you, I love you,*" over and over I felt the Lord's presence for the first time since Tom died. Jesus was trying to love me and tears were streaming down my face. I wanted to go to the altar and just weep, but I didn't want to disrupt the service. Pastor Walker began to speak and talked about how we are bound by many things. He named being afraid to do something different as one of them. I wondered what would have happened if I had gone to the altar in the middle of Kathy's song. In the church where Tom and I had gone before we did that sort of thing, and if someone knelt at the altar during a worship service another member often followed to pray with him.

Pastor finished his sermon and asked everyone to come to the altar so he could lay hands on them and pray. Ushers dimmed the lights and all of the fifteen or so in attendance gathered at the altar. It was the first time I had knelt there without Tom beside me and I felt weak. Pastor laid hands on each one praying for God's healing power, and I sensed the Lord closer than ever before and He was reaching for me. At the same time I felt close to Tom and heard his words echoing in my heart from another Church service.

"Touched by the Holy Ghost in the Lutheran Church," Tom said grinning.

Tom saw my tears that morning and knew the Lord was touching me through the words of a song. I visualized him kneeling there beside me, watching my tears, and praising God for helping me. Yearning to be with Tom, I tried to open my hard heart to receive God's love, but I couldn't release the anger. I was overwhelmed. I had a meltdown and left the altar sobbing.

There was no dismissal after Pastor prayed; everyone just slowly walked out in the dark as the bell tolled. I stood in the pew bawling and Kathy came and put her arms around me.

Driving home I could not stop the tears, even though I kept telling myself I had to get through this. I recited the words from Job, "Man that is born of a woman is of few days and full of trouble." It's our warning not to expect this life to be easy. I cried all the way home, weary of the pain waiting in every corner of my world.

I am lonely tonight. I miss the peace and security of Tom's love.

Friday, April 16, 2004 – 5 months later

Last night I dreamed about Tom for the second time since his death, and it felt as if I was actually with him...

> Standing in the kitchen I glanced out the front door and saw Tom's truck on the carport. "He's home!" I thought, "He's not really gone after all!" My heart was racing, and then I heard footsteps coming down the hallway. "It's Tom!" I told myself. "He always uses the basement door when he's been working in his woodshop or outside." I ran to the doorway and there he was. Before he could say a word I threw my arms around his neck and clung to him with all my might. I couldn't let go.
>
> Dressed in his old blue jeans and dirty sneakers, Tom tried to loosen my grip. "I'm glad you're so happy to see me," he said, "but I've just been outside working in the yard."
>
> I still wouldn't let go. Tom was baffled, convinced he'd been there all the time. He had no concept of the months we'd been apart or the debilitating pain that consumed my every waking moment. His life had simply gone on uninterrupted. Without words, Tom's gentle strength told me everything was alright, and there in his arms I could almost believe it too.

Then the alarm clock brought me back to reality – it was time to get up. In those few seconds between hearing the alarm and actually being awake, I thought Tom was still here with me. When I realized it was just a dream I cried from somewhere so deep I couldn't catch my breath.

Full consciousness ushered in the dark cloud that hovers over my world now, and I just lay there crushed under the weight of sorrow. The dream was so real, I felt like I'd been with Tom. Through the tears, I was strangely comforted. Tom is close now, just a breath away, and his life goes on.

❧❧

I had several dreams about Tom in the first two years of grief, each one more real than the last, and when I woke up reality overwhelmed me. I longed for the few ordinary minutes we shared every day for twenty-five years. I'm convinced God sent these dreams to help me find hope to go on, because in all of them Tom is more alive, more real than my life now. I began to understand how temporary life on earth is and how eternity looks without the constraints of time. Through these dreams of Tom the Lord helped me find strength and hope.

I dreamed I knew Tom was dying. I didn't want him to know he was so sick, but he was digging a hole in the yard with posthole diggers and pushing himself. Worried he would overexert, I tried everything to stop him but he would not quit. I could tell my nagging was getting on his nerves, and finally he turned to me with a stern look and said, "Just let me live until I die."

And so he did. Tom lived every day of his life just as he wanted until the minute he died. This dream helped me to release the guilt I felt about Tom overdoing it on the treadmill that night, and about his working so hard every day.

In another dream I walked into the living room and saw Tom sitting on the couch watching television with his son John and his dad, who died in 2000. My dad, also deceased, was along with some other people sitting in the dining room. I was so excited to see Tom. He glanced up at me as if he had been there all morning and nothing was out of the ordinary. I motioned for him to come over by me and when he did I asked him just to hold me. We walked back to our bedroom and stood in the walk-in closet. Tom put his arms around me, held me for awhile, and kissed my neck. This time we both knew he had died and we talked about how his death took us by surprise. I really felt like I touched Tom that morning and literally talked to him.

When I woke up and realized I had been dreaming, even though the pain returned, I was able to pray without anger. I thanked God for letting Tom hold me. The dream gave me a sense that Heaven is close, even in our midst.

On another occasion I dreamed Tom called me on the phone to tell me he was going downtown to get a haircut. It was like any other day when we called if one of us was running late. Tom was just letting me know where he was so I wouldn't worry.

I dreamed Tom was lying beside me in our bed, propped up on one elbow looking down at me. We'd been talking and enjoying a lazy morning sleeping in. He kissed me, and then for a moment he looked into my eyes with a solemn stance. "You know," Tom said, "He's trying to help you."

I knew Tom was talking about Jesus. I had felt Him reach for me several times, and in anger I rejected Him. Still, He loved me. I already knew Jesus wanted to help me, but when Tom reminded me through the dream it somehow brought me closer to the Lord and gave me the undeniable sense that Tom was with Him.

Another time I dreamed I was with Debbie and Brenda at some kind of gathering with food and a speaker. When I looked around I saw Tom there. He was more of a subtle presence this time, and I walked over and sat down with him. We ate, and then Debbie and I left while Tom was still there. Driving away I said, "I'm glad Tom was there. I couldn't stop staring at him."

The dream was so comforting. Tom and I talked calmly, and I didn't feel the desperate need to cling to him this time. He told me I should go see a widow whose husband had just died, and I was surprised he knew about her.

This time when I woke up I didn't sense that Tom was gone or it was just a dream, but rather that he is near while I keep going on with my daily life. I finally realized I don't have to let him go, and knowing Tom will always be a part of me brought peace.

I dreamed I was in a church service where I did not recognize the building or the pastor. When it came time to leave after the sermon, the pastor sent a man over to plow my fields. What fields? There are no fields at my house, but in my dream there were fields all around my house and it appeared they had not been plowed for awhile. So, the man came with a big tractor to plow my fields, but I wasn't sure if I should let him. I wanted to wait and ask Tom, but I let him plow everything except the fields Tom had planted. After he finished and left, Tom came walking into the kitchen just coming home from work the way he had for the last twenty-five years.

"I had the fields plowed," I told him.

"I see that," he said, "A piece of that pie would be good. Rub my back."

It was just another average day in our life, as if Tom had never been gone. He never did tell me what he thought about the fields, but I got to touch him and talk to him. Then I just started to rub his back and the alarm woke me.

I feel like the Lord is telling me something with the plowing, because when I woke up I pondered on "plowing my fields" with the words "fallow ground" stuck in my mind. So I looked up "fallow" to see what Webster said... *Fallow: land plowed but not seeded for one or more growing seasons, to kill weeds, make the soil richer, etc.* Then I looked up Scripture about "fallow ground" and found two: Jeremiah 4:3 – *"For thus saith the Lord to the men of Judah and Jerusalem, break up your fallow ground and sow not among thorns."* Hosea 10:12 – *"Sow to yourselves in righteousness, reap in mercy; break up your fallow ground; for it is time to seek he Lord till He come and rain righteousness upon you."*

After this dream I tried to seek the Lord because He seemed to be speaking to me through it. Since Tom died everything I ever believed, thought, or knew has been tested. I can no longer accept any doctrine without deep consideration. Whatever the dream was about, God let me talk to Tom and touch him. So real—more real than my life now.

I also dreamed Tom was sitting beside me in some sort of garage after my car had been stolen. We were just talking about things in general the way we used to, and I told him about all the problems I'd been dealing with. I asked him what I should do about the car, but he didn't tell me. What he did say made me think there are progressions in Heaven.

"I have my own things to take care of," Tom said in a busy tone of voice, and by his expression I knew he was involved in activities that were challenging.

This dream reminded me that I have to finish my life, my purpose, and it is mine alone. This life is just the beginning and Heaven is a continuation. The dream was so realistic I turned the porch light on as soon as I woke up to see if my car was still there.

ॐ≪

When I wake up from these dreams it takes a minute for me to face reality again because it feels as though I've been with Tom. In the depth of my being I know Tom still lives and, since there is no time in Heaven, no doubt to him it has only been a few minutes since he left. I remind myself we all have to die, and because Jesus conquered death it is a mere change of address for us. Life goes on. I imagine Tom happy and healthy doing all the things he loved and in spite of the sadness I'm thankful he made it. Tom finished the race, kept the faith, and went to Heaven without suffering pain at his death. It was the perfect exit for him.

After Tom died I kept beating myself up with the "what ifs". What if I would have gotten Tom to take more time off, work less, and relax more? Now I am able to accept the fact that this is just who Tom was, and he would not have been happy any other way. Tom's worst fear was of being an invalid unable to care for himself. Knowing he simply stopped breathing and went to Heaven without suffering soothes my heart. When I think of Tom now, because of these dreams, I can picture him doing all the things he loved without ever getting tired or running out of time.

Tom can't come back, but Jesus gave me these dreams showing Tom's life now to help me go on. There is never an hour when I don't think about Tom and miss him terribly; nevertheless, I am learning minute by minute to find my way through life without him. The dreams helped me deal with the grief by allowing me a glimpse of true reality – Tom's life now. I don't believe Tom sits in Heaven all day on a cloud, plucking a harp or eating cream cheese bagels. He doesn't even like cream cheese that much. I believe Tom is doing the things he loves in a Place where time does not exist. I believe we continue to learn and use our mind and abilities in Heaven. We don't become a different person at death and forget all we knew. Instead, I believe we just continue on unhindered by the limitations and obstacles we have here. Tom has a new body, but he is still Tom. Actually, he's even more himself than he has ever been, because now he is the person God made him to be with all of the negative influences of this life removed. He would not want me to be sad about that.

Each dream of Tom was a part of my healing and a treasure to me. I quickly entered them into my journal so I wouldn't forget the details. Journaling has been a great tool for me for I could read entries made on a better day over and over to draw strength, and on the days I couldn't bear to get out of bed, writing it down seemed to help me release the pain for a time. Reading the journal entries showed progress in my healing, even though it was often one step forward and two steps back.

Wednesday, July 23, 2004 – 8 months later, Tom's birthday

Today is Tom's birthday. A looming sadness invades my every memory of him, a sorrow deepened by the funeral earlier today for my cousin Emma who committed suicide.

Only 56, she seemed to have so much to live for, a son, two daughters, and grandchildren. Standing behind her youngest daughter at the gravesite, I watched as her entire body trembled throughout the service. I wondered what she was thinking. Was she already tormented by the "Whys?" and "What ifs?" Was the loss compounded because her mom chose to leave them? The Pastor read *The Lord's Prayer* in closing and, as we filed down the hill to our cars, bagpipes played a haunting *Amazing Grace.* I thought of Tom...

Sitting by his grave for the funeral that cold November day, we cried for Tom, for the times we had and for those we'd miss, but we never considered he would want to leave us. He tried so hard to live, too hard in fact. If he hadn't pushed so much so fast after his stent surgery, he might still be here. Somehow, even though I was surrounded by immense pain, knowing how much Tom wanted to stay comforted me.

Driving home I played Tom's Conway Twitty CD and stopped at McDonald's for fries to snack on, the way he always did when we were out and about. Since Tom died, I often find myself doing things he would do. It seems to give footing to my life that's been swept into the abyss. In twenty-five years with Tom I never washed the car or worked in the yard, yet now I have a nagging compulsion to keep the car clean and the yard looking nice the way he did. I even find myself using his little quips. For instance, last week when David hung the new corner shelf in our sunroom I said, "I'm gonna put our picture on one shelf and Granma's pitcher on the other." With my southern accent picture and pitcher are barely distinguishable.

Tom would chuckle. "We only have one pitcher", he'd say.

Today those memories make me cry, but one day they will be sweet reminders of twenty-five perfect years with a special man who loved me.

Maybe tonight I'll have a big, juicy, medium rare steak for supper and a piece of chocolate cake to celebrate Tom and the day God sent love to the Wilhelm family.

෧෧

Grief is unrelenting. It's a crouching black panther poised to attack the moment I wake in the morning, and then it stalks every segment of my day. There is no hiding place, no time out. Hour after hour, day after day, month after month I feel the claws digging into my soul. Others don't know, they can't see. Emotions don't bleed so the deep gashes are invisible. They still believe the funeral was the hardest part and after a few weeks things would be fine. They have no clue about grief's reality, or the way a weary soul welcomes even death to find relief.

The funeral service for my cousin was a turning point for me. Until I saw the pain in the faces of her children, sisters, and friends, I had been selfish in my desire to go with Tom. Until I saw her nine-year-old twin granddaughters sobbing by her casket at visitation, I had not considered those left behind to grieve for me. I left the cemetery with a new perspective. I could no longer just wait to die. Somehow, I had to find the courage to live.

A bit of a pessimist, I often struggle with depression and thoughts about death. In those early months I remember praying, "Lord, I just want to stop breathing. Don't make me stay here without Tom."

Many times I cried until I could hardly breathe, aware of how fragile life really is. Tom was fine, and then he was gone. It could be that way with me. It is not uncommon for elderly surviving spouses to die soon after the loss. Grief is hard, even life-changing, and those left behind suffer. It's a part of life.

Watching my cousin's family, I imagined my death. Who would mourn for me? I pictured myself in a casket with visitors filing by for one last goodbye. In my mind a mental list began to form of lives that would be altered with my death, of those who would miss me...I thought about my daughter. What if Christy had a bad day and needed to talk? What about my friends? Would Debbie and Brenda still meet every Tuesday for quilting without me? Would my church friends that meet at my house every Wednesday from June to September for potluck and a Bible study continue on without me in a new place? Would Barbra miss having lunch with me once a week? What about my bosses? And the list goes on.

Rehearsing these relationships in my mind and thinking about their pain after my death gave me strength to take another step forward. Tom didn't want to die and leave the people he loved, but death is inevitable. Life is a gift – this hour, this moment—and while it is not all sunshine and roses, we are not alone in the hard places. Family and friends are close to love and help us, and one Friend has even promised never to leave. Moreover, according to Psalms 34:18, "The Lord is close to the brokenhearted and saves those who are crushed in spirit."

Nothing can stop the sorrow of losing those we love, but there is solace in holding onto the ones we still have.

Thursday, August 12, 2004 – 9 months later

Tonight I had a tea party in my sunroom for the friends who have walked with me through grief. I served homemade pimento cheese sandwiches, fresh peach cream cheese delight, and of course, tea. It was my first dinner party without Tom and, since entertaining was something we did together, it made me miss him. Tom was always here to help me cook and clean up.

Last night I stood alone in the kitchen, nervous and stressed, struggling to put the shredder attachment on the mixer. Tom always put it together and I had never tried to do it. Now it was after ten and I still had not made the pimento cheese. Frustrated, I sat down at the table and wanted to cry, but I didn't. I couldn't give up. If I did, I would keep giving up instead of pressing to find my way back to life. I found the instructions and tried once more to assemble it. Thirty minutes later the part snapped into place.

Everyone I invited came, all those who placed a shoulder under my load when drawing my next breath seemed more than I could manage. It was a good night, although pimento cheese seemed a poor feast to serve to angels.

&ro&

It seems people are always at a loss when it comes to knowing what to say or do for those in grief. I'm always aware of how uncomfortable it is for others, especially married couples, to be with me now. They know one day one of them will be where I am, a reality nobody wants to consider.

I have been blessed with a circle of friends who reach out to me through the invisible wall of despair. In spite of the tears they invite me over, ask me to a movie, or stop by for coffee. These special friends carried light into my endless night and helped me see the road ahead.

Rabbi Kushner says in his book, *When Bad Things Happen to Good People,* "People are God's language." [2]

Eight months ago Tom took his last breath and, although I couldn't stop breathing, I was sure I could not keep living. Then, my friends carried me. They didn't know what to do or say, so they just sat with me for awhile and listened. Those visits, calls, cards, and e-mails held me to life and I could not have made it without the special gift of their time and love.

Sunday, September 19, 2004 – 10 months later

It's Sunday and I'm still not back in church, still can't pray, still angry with God. Where is my faith? Where is the strong Christian I believed I was?

Sundays are the hardest times for me because it was our day to play. After Church, Tom would stop at the CIT-GO on the edge of town for gas and a Snickers bar to split, then he'd find a back road to escape traffic. We took long drives to the lake or through the mountains into Cades Cove, talking and taking in the views. We often saw a deer or bear in the woods along the way. It seems so long ago now, was that really my life?

It's quiet this morning and the house seems emptier than usual. I poured myself a cup of coffee, tuned the television to channel four and lowered the volume like Tom always did before sitting down to read the newspaper. It was all too familiar and the memories were crushing me, so I turned the television off and put some compact discs on to play. One was by Josh Groban and when he sang *To Where You Are*, I broke...

> *"Who can say for certain, maybe you're still here. I feel you all around me, your memories so clear. Deep in the stillness I can hear you speak. You're still an inspiration. Can it be you are my forever love and you are watching over me from up above? Fly me up to where you are, beyond the distant star I wish upon tonight to see you smile, if only for a while to know you're there. A breath away is not far to where you are."[3]*

Listening to his words brought Tom close, and I just stood in the doorway sobbing until I was gasping for breath. "Maybe I *will* stop breathing," I thought. I didn't want to breathe anymore. I didn't want to live anymore. I just wanted to go with Tom.

Suddenly, I sensed the Lord's presence. He was there, just as He had been so many times during the previous months in my darkest hours. He kept coming to me even though I rejected Him, yet when I begged Him to help me that night, He didn't come. Tom died. Now here He was, standing, waiting, and reaching for me. I felt so weak and broken, so alone. Even so, I remembered the closeness I once had with Jesus. I knew the hiding place in Him. Unable to resist any longer, I turned toward the Lord. He wrapped me in His love and the anger melted away. Tired, weak, and lonely I just rested in the safety of His arms for a moment.

Recalling the words of Isaiah 53:3, *"He was a man of sorrows, and acquainted with grief,"* I sensed a compassion born of His own pain. I reflected for a moment on the shortest verse in the Bible, *"Jesus wept"* (John 11:33), trying to understand why Jesus would weep over the death of Lazarus when He was there to raise him from the dead. Then I saw it, the truth of that Scripture...Jesus did not weep for Lazarus; His tears were for Mary and Martha. When Jesus saw their pain, He felt it too. Today He cried with me.

Wednesday, September 22, 2004 – 10 months later

"Cathy!" I heard someone call out as I walked through the church doors tonight on my way to Griefshare. Scanning the lobby I saw Deborah waving and smiling at me from across the entrance hall.

I met Deborah three months ago when she sat down beside me at the first Griefshare meeting. At forty-nine, I considered myself a young widow but Deborah looked much younger. Until we introduced ourselves, I supposed she had come for help with grieving the loss of a parent, then I found out her husband died at forty-two from a malignant brain tumor.

It was time for the session to start when Patsy walked in and took the seat next to Deborah. Here was an assembly with one common thread, all were newly widowed. In that first meeting I was visibly angry, Patsy tried to be strong, and Deborah cried the whole hour. We could not have foreseen the deep lasting bond that would grow from our shared sorrow.

"I brought this for you," Deborah said, handing me a book. "It's about Heaven and it really helped me."

We are all obsessed about Heaven now. What is it like? What are our husbands doing? Any comfort we find is like cold water to a parched tongue and we can't wait to share it. As Deborah's words of hope flowed into my heart I could not wait to tell her my news.

"I've let go of my anger," I said.

"You don't have to tell me," she said. "I can see you're different."

Every Wednesday night for the past three months Deborah sat beside me, watching my expressions, listening to the venom spew out my anger toward God. Week after week she and the others hoped I would find peace and now, as she listened to my story, I saw her happy tears. Her genuine love and concern went straight into my heart.

I felt hopeless and alone after Tom died, isolated and abandoned by God. Satan aims to convince us nobody cares and his scheme worked well with me, until now.

Deborah and I walked in together and took our seats at the table. Six smiling faces were glad to see me, and I was certain each one cared about me and wanted me to be whole. Their support had become my safe place. Like a squadron of wounded soldiers, each one maimed by a grenade blast, we tried desperately to help each other. The tiniest step forward for one was a major victory for all, and tonight we celebrated.

෨෯

We attended weekly Griefshare sessions for six months, but the friendship between Deborah, Patsy, and I reached beyond the group. We planned nights out together to have dinner, see a movie, or just hang out and talk. We saw Tammy Trent in concert, treated ourselves to a manicure and pedicure, and visited the graves of our husbands. Deborah gave us a Josh Groban CD with *To Where You Are* and we drove around one evening in her vehicle after Griefshare listening to it and sobbing in unison. When one of us sank too low the others were there to buoy her up.

We joined a women's Sunday school class and one Sunday morning as we were leaving Deborah saw me crying. Knowing I was having a hard day, Deborah didn't want me to be alone so she skipped Church and we went to Shoney's for brunch.

Deborah came to my rescue on another day when I was going down. She wasn't home to answer my call, but I left a message for her before I jumped in the car to ramble around for awhile. Sometimes, when it gets too sad, it helps to get out of the house and do something. Shopping is a good diversion but when you are depressed it is easy to overspend or buy on impulse. Once I went to Wal-Mart to escape the pain and came home with five pairs of sandals.

I drove to the mall and had just walked into Catos and started browsing when my cell phone rang.

"Cathy," Deborah said, "where are you?"

"I'm at Catos," I said, "spending money I don't have, buying things I don't need."

"You ok?" she asked, knowing the answer already.

"No," I said, "this has been a bad day and I could not stay home alone any longer, so I came to the mall."

"Do you want to meet me somewhere and get a burger?" she asked.

"Yes," I said through tears.

Deborah met me at a restaurant close to the mall and we talked for over an hour. She shared my load and helped me find the strength for one more day.

Thursday, September 30, 2004—10 months later

Barbra and I planned to meet at Patriot Park after work to walk, but it started pouring rain as we pulled into the parking lot. It seemed rational to cancel our walk and wait for a clearer day, but Barbra knew how much I depended on her support.

"What do you think?" Barbra asked. "Do you want to walk?"

"Do you?" I asked.

"If you do," she said.

"Maybe for a little while," I said grabbing the umbrella.

It had been a tough day and, for no apparent reason, fear was creeping in. I wanted Barbra to stay with me, but I hated being so needy. Barbra makes my problems her own and doesn't stop until we find a solution. Moreover, she constantly lets me know that Jesus is standing here wanting to help me. I guess I needed to hear that today.

We set out on our first lap, when everyone else was making their way to the car and out of the rain. We walked and talked, while I cried, which must have seemed strange to those walking passed us. Alone on the track, our feet soaking wet, we kept walking until I was able to go home.

⮞⬸

Growing up Barbra lived next door to me and we shared the same birthday, except I am one year older. We played dolls, made mud pies, and even set the woods on fire playing with matches before she moved away when I was about ten years old. Through the years we have lost track of each other at times, but some crisis would eventually bring us back together. After Tom's funeral, Barbra told me she thought it was time we stayed in contact more. I agreed, and now we have lunch together once a week.

With Barbra I am still a kid and we do silly things, like watching the Garfield movie, driving to Sonic for a mini banana split, or sharing a watermelon. One night Barbra invited me for supper, and afterwards she sent me home with an orange moon pie and guacamole dip. I'm free to be me with Barbra, and I know she loves me. If I called her at three in the morning on a work day, I know she would come.

Friday, October 15, 2004 – 11 months later

It was still dark outside when Christy pulled in the driveway to set up for our yard sale. Even though we advertised eight a.m. we knew some would come early, especially men interested in the tools we listed. Christy rounded up the calculator, pen and pad, along with the shoebox with our money for change, and then took her seat behind the checkout table. She loves yard sales and is much faster than I am at taking money, so she was in charge of sales while I worked to keep things organized.

It was a busy morning as strangers shuffled through Tom's things—his woodworking tools and books, back issues of *Handyman*, die cast toys, and other collectibles. They bumped into the old barrel he found at the antique store one Saturday when we drove to Black Mountain. It was the perfect accessory Tom needed to complete his ship room. Every item for sale held a memory, even the old wringer washing machine Tom spotted at the flea market on our drive back from Ohio.

"This is exactly what they used at the car wash back in the sixties," Tom said. I saw the sparkle in his eye that appeared every time he talked about trucks. We paid ninety-five dollars for that rusty little tub on wheels, but it was a treasure to Tom. He used it every Saturday to wash his truck and wring out his shammy.

It was hard to watch them touch Tom's things and treat them so carelessly. Amid the shoppers I noticed a young woman looking through Tom's woodworking books.

"My husband was a woodworker," I said, "and he had lots of patterns."

"I only have five dollars," she replied studying three books in her hands, "and I can't decide which one to get for my husband. He is just getting started in woodworking."

I had priced each book at five dollars, but I knew the value to Tom was much more. I stood beside her for a minute reminiscing about the times Tom and I had been in a similar situation during our first years together. "There's a special today," I said. "You can have all three for five dollars." It was my best sale of the day.

We had a successful sale and made more than expected, yet the thrill of our reward was dampened somewhat since every item carried away reminded us Tom was gone. Christy and I packed up our surplus, then treated ourselves to lunch at Red Lobster with the profits.

While we waited for our food, I choked back tears recalling special times I had been there with Tom. Red Lobster was our favorite restaurant and when my thoughts went back to the first time we ordered crab legs, I had to smile. The server sat two plates in front of us piled high with the red-shelled appendages along with tools for cracking.

"Enjoy!" she said as she walked away.

We looked down at our plates then back at each other. "It can't be that hard," Tom said. Always the optimist...

We may have left hungry that night if the server had not walked by our table and observed our futile attempts to extract meat from those long spindly creatures and came to our rescue.

❧❧

Today I was immersed in memories of my life with Tom, a life that no longer exists. People see a new widow and think life will get back to normal after a few months, unaware that for her normal no longer exists. Normal was the day-by-day activities with her husband, simple routines, coffee in the morning, watching the evening news, and weekend chores. Without him everything is different. Now vacations, holidays, and family gatherings will be forever altered and, no matter how much she craves the familiar past, there is no going back. Tomorrow will be a new day, a new normal.

Tom's death was a tornado that blew through my life and swept away not only the present but also the future we'd planned. What now? Did anything survive? I looked across the table at my daughter and calm settled over me. Christy made it out! She survived the storm. With her my life is real. I'm still me, and I know she will be here to help me sort through the rubble.

Monday, November 22, 2004—one year later

It's Monday before Thanksgiving...Can it really have been only a year since Tom died? Is it possible I survived twelve months without him? Just as my thoughts drifted back to the horror of that night, the phone rang and jarred me back to the present. It was Tammy.

"Do you already have plans for tonight?" Tammy asked.

"No," I said, "it's the Monday before Thanksgiving, the first anniversary."

"I know," Tammy said. "If you are going to be home, I thought I would come over."

"Come on," I said. "I am weepy, but I'll be here."

After work, Tammy met me at the cemetery and I exchanged the faded flowers on Tom's grave for a new winter arrangement. Along with the flowers I used a rubber band to attach the following description of success to the vase. Tom was truly successful.

Success

By: Bessie Stanley

He has achieved success who has lived well, laughed often and loved much; who has enjoyed the trust of pure women, the respect of intelligent men and the love of little children; who has filled his niche and accomplished his task; who has left the world better than he found it, whether by an improved poppy, a perfect poem or a rescued soul; who has never lacked appreciation of earth's beauty or failed to express it; who has always looked for the best in others and given them the best he had; whose life was an inspiration; whose memory a benediction.[4]

Tammy followed me home and we sat for the next hour or so talking about Tom. Talking about the deceased makes some persons uncomfortable, but for survivors it offers great comfort. Instead of reliving Tom's death today, Tammy and I remembered his life.

After Tom died, Tammy wanted to buy "Midnight", his truck – the black, four-wheel-drive, club-cab, Dodge Ram with an appearance package direct from the factory. In other words, the truck Tom loved. He loved it so much, in fact, I had to sit and wait for him to go into Wal-Mart the night he bought it, so nobody would steal it while he was inside buying the "Club" for security.

In order to buy Tom's truck, Tammy and David had to sell their Chevy Silverado. One evening when they came to visit, the UPS driver left a package on the carport and Tammy carried it into the kitchen. When I went to pick it up I noticed a plain white envelope lying beside it on the table.

"What's this?" I asked picking up the envelope.

"The UPS guy must have dropped it," Tammy replied.

When I opened the envelope and found it stuffed with hundred dollar bills, I panicked. "How can I get this back to him?" I asked.

Then I saw Tom's grin on Tammy's face and I knew something was up. As it turned out, the money came from the sale of their truck.

Tom was quite a prankster, and so much of him is still here in Tammy.

chapter 4
My Second Year Alone

GOOD FRIDAY, MARCH 25, 2005 – 1 year and 4 months later

Only fourteen people showed up for the Good Friday Service of Darkness tonight and the way they were scattered in the pews made the sanctuary seem deserted.

Attending a church service without Tom is still my biggest hurdle, even though I feel him close there. On two occasions, when the congregation sang *Holy, Holy, Holy* and *What a Friend We Have in Jesus*, I could hear Tom next to me singing along. It was the most beautiful sound I've ever heard, and yet I cried throughout the service.

When I walked in I glanced across the benches and spotted Debbi sitting alone. I didn't know Debbi very well, since she started coming to the Church while I was absent and angry. We met for the first time a few months ago when I came back for a baptismal service on a Wednesday night.

"Can I sit with you?" I asked.

"Sure," Debbi said with a smile.

Glancing at the bulletin I noticed the entire service was singing this year, and none of the songs were familiar. The mood was solemn when we started to sing, with lights dimmed and the altar draped in black. In an assembly of only fourteen voices spread across the Church everyone was audible. Halfway through the first song Debbi and I turned toward each other and grinned. We kept singing but our lack of musical talent was obvious, and we had to stifle the urge to laugh through the rest of the service.

"That was pretty bad," Debbi said as we walked out together. "We should not sit next to each other for singing."

"Yes, I know. We just needed more voices to drown us out," I said. "Have you eaten supper?"

"Not yet," Debbi said.

"Well, if you don't have to go home right away, why don't we go somewhere to eat?" I asked.

"Sounds good," she said. "Where can we go?"

We named several restaurants that sounded good and after a brief discussion settled on Olive Garden. After dinner we sat and talked for over an hour getting to know each other. I told her about losing Tom, and she explained her husband's job loss after twenty-five years that forced them to move, and the circumstances keeping them apart. Although for different reasons, both of us were alone. Since I live close to the restaurant Debbi followed me home and we talked for hours about our lives and how quickly they had changed. Ours was an instant friendship and this the first of many nights out together.

Debbi worked for an area attraction and could get free or discounted admission to many local amusements so, rather than sit home alone every week, we made plans to see some of them. Saturday became our "date night" and we went to a different place every week. We sat through an assimilated hurricane at Wonderworks, watched a pig race at Dixie Stampede, and got a kiss from the Elvis impersonator at Memories Theater. I stood up at Black Bear Jamboree when I heard the announcer say, "Please stand up," then I wondered why only a few others rose with me, excluding Debbi. When the seated patrons saluted those of us standing, it became clearer. Debbi and I were talking and I missed the first part of our instructions, "Will all those who served in the military." It was worth the embarrassment of being called a WAC in the following weeks for both of us to have a good belly laugh. Saturdays held a good deal of laughter for Debbi and me, along with some tears.

If I was sad, Debbi would say, "Look at all the good things you still have in your life, instead of just what you don't have." Then she would point those things out to me.

On nights when Debbi felt discouraged about the future, missing Tim and her old life in Texas, I reminded her the situation is temporary. "Things will work out one day," I said. "You still have Tim and your life with him and that's all that matters."

We found a safe haven in our friendship and at the end of the day we knew we were not alone.

Sunday, December 18, 2005 – 2 years and 1 month later

On my way to Church this morning I turned my radio to the station that plays gospel music on Sunday mornings, the one Tom and I always listened to. I opened my heart hoping the Lord would speak to me in the words of a song. I haven't been able to pray freely since Tom died; the words seem empty when I try. Just as I asked the Lord to help me and give my life direction, *Word of God Speak* by Mercy Me began to play.

> *I'm finding myself at a loss for words and the funny thing is, it's ok. The last thing I need is to be heard, but to hear what You would say to me. Word of God speak. Would You pour down like rain washing my eyes to see your majesty? To be still and know that You're in this place. Please let me stay and rest in your holiness. Word of God speak. I'm finding myself in the midst of You, beyond the music and beyond the noise. All that I need is to be with You and in the quiet to hear Your voice. Word of God speak.[5]*

I felt Jesus near and I began to talk to Him and this time I knew He heard me. I was praying the words of the song because I felt them. I just wanted to be in that safe, quiet place with Jesus where I could find peace and rest and restoration for my soul.

The next song to play was *Thank You* by Ray Boltz, the song Lydia sang at Tom's funeral. It begins, "*I dreamed I went to Heaven and you were there with me,*" and then it lists the ways this person had blessed others when he didn't even know it. One part says, "*Friend, you may not know me now and then he said, but wait, you used to teach my Sunday school when I was only eight and every week you would say a prayer before the class would start and one day when you said that prayer I asked Jesus in my heart.*[6] Tom loved that song but had no idea how much it described his own life. He lived out his faith in the small things he did every day, and I'm sure as people come to Heaven he will hear stories like this. It was over a year before I could listen to this song again and even then it made me cry, but today as I listened something else happened. I thought of how Tom kept the faith and finished his course, and I began to sense that I haven't finished mine. I remember things I had told Jesus throughout the years. Things like, "I'll always love You," and "Though the cost be great I'll work for You." After Tom died, all of that seemed to vanish. I felt abandoned, but this morning I knew Jesus had been there all the while. He still loves me and He has been waiting patiently for me.

The last song I heard just before I walked into church was *Go Light Your World* by Kathy Troccoli. It starts off saying, *"There is a candle in every soul, some brightly burning, some dark and cold. There is a spirit who brings the fire, ignites the candle and makes His home. Carry your candle, run to the darkness, seek out the hopeless, confused and torn. Hold out your candle, go light your world."*[7] I am not sure what that means, but I heard Jesus speaking to my heart and I know He does have a plan for me. While this song played I thought of C.S. Lewis, broken by the death of his wife, yet with his own pain he helped untold numbers of people like me through the dark tunnel of grief. I almost felt guilty because I was so helped by his wounds, and yet it is why he wrote *A Grief Observed*.

As I walked into Church I still felt the Lord's presence. The first song for the congregation was *Here I Am Lord,*[8] which I had never heard before. As we sang the Lord began to speak to me through the lyrics. I heard Him say, *"I have heard my people cry,"* and listened as we sang about the things He wanted to do: *"I will make their darkness bright, I will tend the poor and lame, I will set a feast for them."* Then I heard Him ask, *"Who will bear My light to them? Whom shall I send?"* I remembered the times I had said, "Here I am, Lord, send me." I used to sing a song to the Lord that said, *"Jesus, use me and, oh Lord, don't refuse me for surely there's a work that I can do. And even though it's humble, Lord, help my will to crumble. Though the cost be great I'll work for You."* I have thought about that song many times this year when I asked myself, "Am I giving up? Will I let Satan win?" Today as we sang, *"Here I am Lord, Is it I, Lord? I have heard You calling in the night. I will go Lord, if You lead me. I will hold your people in my heart,"* I cried and wanted to raise my hand.

I did hear the Lord calling in the night during that first few months of grief while I was still angry with Him. I woke up sobbing in the middle of the night and felt Jesus close. He said, "If you will follow Me, I will make you a fisher of men." Today I stood in God's presence and, while I may not know what it all means or the direction to take, I know Him and I know His voice.

chapter 5
Finding My Way Back

SUNDAY, FEBRUARY 12, 2006 – 2 years, 3 months later

Today Kathy and I drove back from a Lutheran weekend retreat in Atlanta, Georgia called "Catch the Spirit". It was a chance to get away with a friend for the weekend and my opportunity to escape grief for a day or two. Having no expectations, I never suspected the divine appointment God had arranged for me there.

I finally worked through my anger with God and started back to church last year, but I'm just occupying space there. I have no sense of direction or purpose and I just can't seem to find my way back. I'm convinced God loves me and He did not take Tom to punish me, so why am I still so lost? Tom and I were active in church for twenty-five years—always together, always a team. He was my best friend, my confidant, my rock. Now the pews hold vivid memories of him, weights that press on my heart with every beat. This retreat, I thought, would be a new and unfamiliar place, safe from the memories. If I'd only known what lay ahead...

A workshop, *Simply Pray,* caught our attention as we scanned the itinerary offered at "Catch the Spirit", and it was about time for it to start in the chapel. Like freshmen on the first day of school we scurried through the hallways. We were the first ones to enter the tiny chapel lit only by candles scattered on the floor in front of the altar. The atmosphere demanded our respect and we quickly took on a more serious tone. No instructor waited by the door to greet us or hand out pamphlets like the other sessions.

"Are you sure we're in the right place?" I whispered to Kathy.

She pulled out the itinerary and confirmed, "That's what it says."

We found a seat and waited. Time to start drew nearer and the chapel was almost full. Still, no instructor. Puzzled, we all sat in silence wondering what would happen. Then, without introduction, a young man in the front row began singing, almost chanting, a short soothing chorus. He repeated the chorus three times then quoted Jeremiah 29:11, *"For I know the plans I have for you", declares the Lord, "Plans to prosper you and not to harm you, plans to give you hope and a future."* Tears flooded my eyes as I remembered how often we'd used these words for comfort in GriefShare. It had become our group's unofficial motto.

The young man began to sing a different chorus now, repeating it three times. Then, after a brief pause, he read the story of the prodigal son from Luke, Chapter 15. One passage pierced my heart – *And when he was yet a great way off, his father saw him, and had compassion and ran and fell on his neck, and kissed him.* I thought about those early months after Tom died and how lost I felt. Even a year later, after I came back to church, I was *"yet a great way off."* I felt Jesus close. He found me in that little chapel. I tried to stifle the sobs as He came running to me and wrapped me in His love.

The young man didn't get up or look around, he just asked us to listen as he read a second time.

"See if any part of the Scripture seems to leap out at you," he instructed.

As he read the second time, those same words gripped my heart, *"And while he was yet a great way off."* After another pause, he asked us to rest and contemplate what God might be trying to say to us. Then he read the third time.

The Lord felt so close. Everyone sat silently, awed by His presence. The young man sang yet another chorus three times. Then he got up, walked toward the door, and turned on the lights.

"Welcome to *Simply Pray*," he said, reaching for his handouts. "I am Eric Murray, Pastor of Messiah Lutheran in Knoxville, Tennessee."

Pastor Murray concluded the session with a discussion on prayer using quotes from various sources. By using the illustration of a small child climbing upon his father's lap to describe prayer, he reminded us our Heavenly Father wants to spend time with us.

"Whether it's to bandage a skinned knee, hide from a mean dog, or just feel safe," he explained, "there is no wrong reason to come to our Father and no wrong words to say."

Finally, Pastor Murray invited us to share our own unique ways of praying, and the responses varied with each individual. One man explained how in his lowest moments he silently lifts his empty palm to Jesus to signify his need. I was so moved by his sharing I too began to pray with no words. In times when pain was too deep to express I'd lift my empty palm to Jesus, giving it to Him.

Our time was up. The session ended but nobody moved. We were basking in the warmth of God's love and didn't want to stop. Slowly everyone began to stroll out until the room was empty.

Kathy and I couldn't stop talking about our experience in the chapel that day and how it changed us. We even tried to recreate *"Simply Pray"* in a mid-week service for our congregation at home.

This short workshop was a turning point for me. It brought me closer to the heart of God. I left Atlanta knowing I have a Heavenly Father who loves me so much He will run to me if I will only turn toward Him. Now when it feels like my life is over I know He has a plan for me—a plan for good and a future. Losing Tom left such an empty space it often feels like the end of my life too, but God still has a plan for me. Somewhere in the midst of the unbearable grief I found new hope. *I am not alone. My life is not over. I have a future.*

This weekend I took one more step forward.

ॐ∼

Divine appointments, those unexpected rendezvous with someone you did not expect to see in a place you seldom go. You find yourself in the right place at the precise time to encounter a special blessing, and there is no doubt that God arranged the meeting. During the months I was away from Church, God sent my Church family to me.

Lisa was in line at the Post Office when I stopped in to mail a package, and as soon as she saw me she put her arms around my neck and just held on.

"I don't want to let go," Lisa said.

"I never come to this Post Office," I said choking back tears, "but I ran an errand for work and passed by it. Now I'm glad I stopped."

My guilty conscience for skipping Church all those months made me shrink back when I caught sight of a member, for fear he would ask where I had been. That thought crossed my mind one Sunday afternoon when I saw Lisa again in the Mexican food section in Kroger. I could have darted in the next aisle to avoid her, but then I remembered the hug.

"Hey there," Lisa said, "I'm so glad to see you. How are you?"

"This has been a tough day, and I just left the cemetery," I said. "I took flowers for Tom."

Lisa's tears displayed true compassion, and we cried together as she told me about losing her dad to cancer at a young age.

A few weeks later at a local concert, Don and Betty occupied the seats behind me. They were friends of ours from Church and Don had been a pall bearer for Tom. I hadn't noticed them until I felt a tap on my shoulder and turned around to see two happy faces smiling back at me. Next came the hugs, and then we talked nonstop until the concert began.

One evening after I decided to change the color of my kitchen, I went to Lowe's to buy paint and I heard someone call my name from across the store. When I looked around I saw Bill and Shirley hurrying toward me beaming with excitement to see me. They were also our friends from Church, and Bill too was a pall bearer for Tom. We even talked about taking a trip together before Tom died. They were there shopping for poinsettias for the Church but stopped long enough to give me hugs.

My sister Peggy and I often meet at Patriot Park after work to walk because it is on our route home. Every now and then when Peggy has the day off or goes home early, we walk at Sevierville City Park. It is more convenient from home for both of us. Without fail, every time we walked the Sevierville track we came upon Robin wearing her "Lutheran Chicks" sweatshirt. Time and again Robin sent elaborate cards to me with beautiful handwritten messages, and each time I bumped into her at the park she interrupted her walk to give me a don't-want-to-let-go hug.

Every hug from a Church member was God's arms pulling me closer. When I finally resumed regular Church attendance, at least five hugs met me in the narthex every Sunday morning as soon as I walked through the door, and I never sat alone. Once, I was despondent and tried to slip in unnoticed. I took a seat in the back pews, but Don saw me there alone and came to sit with me. I was home.

Sunday, October 15, 2006—2 years and 11 months later

I just got home from three days at Via de Cristo, a Lutheran retreat. I went to Via de Cristo hoping to encounter Jesus in a close-up and personal way and find direction for my life. I did not come away disappointed. Every part of the weekend was a time of refreshing, as I watched God's perfectly orchestrated plan come together.

After Tom died I closed up—couldn't pray, didn't want to. Jesus kept loving me all the same and drawing me to Himself. *Simply Pray* in Atlanta is one example. When Pastor Murray read about the prodigal son, I felt Jesus running toward me with arms outstretched, wanting to love me. Then one Sunday morning in Church, while I was sitting in the pew, just occupying space really, I felt dead and empty, and then Jesus came close. It was as if I kept sinking in quicksand with Him lying on the ground straining to reach me and pull me back, and I would not give Him my hand. That day I decided I had to try again.

I went online to find the website for Via de Cristo and signed up. Present at the retreat were Christians from all denominations, and yet I have never experienced such unity. Through prayer God brought His people together in this place for a purpose—one purpose—to help us on our journey. From the speaker, to the one beside you at breakfast, to the one you bumped into in the hall, every part of the weekend was a special surprise for us from Heaven.

We cannot see the bigger picture, but somehow we have to find faith to trust that our Heavenly Father loves us and is working for our good. I left Via de Cristo knowing we do indeed matter to God and He does hear and answer prayer. He will never leave us nor forsake us. *If I ascend up into Heaven, Thou are there; if I make my bed in Hell, behold, Thou are there. (Psalms 139:8)* Jesus spoke to me through the words of a song, *Borning Cry.*[9] *"I was there to hear your borning cry, I'll be there when you are old,"* He said. Jesus was there with me that night, He was with Tom as he began walking free, and He will be with me until this life comes to an end.

I feel a stirring in my spirit and, no doubt, the plan God has always had for my life is unfolding even through the struggles, and His healing is taking place. Now I hold onto His promises as an anchor for my life: *For I know the plans I have for you, plans for good and not for disaster, to give you hope and a future (Jeremiah 29:11). And lo, I am with you always, even until the end of the world (Matthew 28:20).*

Tuesday, February 6, 2007—3 years and 3 months later

The Lord brought me a special blessing tonight. I was sitting in the recliner watching television and glanced over at Tom's empty chair. Memories carried me back to an evening I spent with him and, as we sat together with a cup of coffee watching the six o'clock news, I reached over and patted Tom's arm.

"I love you too much," I said.

"Why?" Tom asked.

"Just because," I said.

Yearning to be near Tom, I dug out the box where I stowed his personal items after the funeral and rummaged through it again. I touched his watch, his glasses, the box cutter in a leather sheath that hung from his belt, his pocket knife, and his wallet with pictures still tucked into cloudy sleeves. I found the old snapshot of me Tom carried with him for twenty years. He thought I looked sexy. Bent and faded, it had captured Tom's love for me, and when I turned it over to check for a date, there it was—my blessing. Behind that old photo of me was Tom's half of our "Mizpah".

The first year of our marriage I bought a gold Mizpah charm divided in halves, one half for Tom and one for me. When the two halves were joined together an engraved prayer appeared, which was taken from Genesis 31: 49, *"May the Lord keep watch between me and thee when we are apart."*

I always wrote prayers to the Lord, especially if I was deeply troubled or in dire need. Most of the time I put the prayer between our mattresses in case I forgot to pray about it that night. It helped me to know God had it in writing. Debbie found this quip in the newspaper and thought of me, "Nothing is really said until it's documented." The Mizpah was our written prayer, my half for Tom, and his for me.

When Tom died he no longer needed my prayer, but I desperately need his. I don't think Tom knows anything about me now, except what the Lord shows him, but I do believe he prays for me. The rich man who lifted up his eyes in Hell asked someone to go talk to his brothers so they would not come to that terrible place, and that tells me we are aware of those left behind. I am sure Tom is asking God to help me now.

More often than not I feel lost and alone, disengaged from day to day life. It feels like the world I knew vanished and the life Tom and I had was lost and forgotten. Then once in a while there is a window of hope, when I know God is holding both Tom and me and we don't seem so far apart. When I found the Mizpah I sensed the Lord's presence and I felt safe and protected. He came to tell me that Tom and I are separated and, just as when we were apart on earth, He is still watching between us. In Him we are still one and He has not forgotten our life.

When Tom died I emptied his wallet searching for his half of the Mizpah prayer, but I couldn't find it. Tonight, when I turned that picture over, it was as if Jesus handed me a tiny gold charm carrying Tom's prayer straight from Heaven.

Friday, January 18, 2008—4 years, 2 months later

After work today I hurried to the Music Road Hotel to hear a lecture by Fred Alsop at the Wilderness Wildlife Week. Dr. Alsop, field biologist, avid birder and author of *Birds of the Smokies*, mesmerized the group with his presentation. In closing, He invited those present to accompany him on a birding expedition to Cades Cove tomorrow from 7:45 am until 2:00 pm. Twenty people could go and the sign-up sheet was out front. I felt an excitement come over me that I thought was gone for good. I stopped going to Cades Cove when Tom died because painful memories blocked its beauty.

This eleven-mile motor nature loop in the Great Smoky Mountains National Park was our favorite place to go on Sundays after church. We stopped at the little market for some broasted chicken before entering the Park, and then half way around the loop we found a quiet spot to pull off for a picnic. We enjoyed the view while we ate chicken and waited for deer to come out into the open.

Now, after 4 years, I wanted to go again. Could it really have been 4 years? I paused for a minute to take the test, the new life test. Was this something I wanted to do because I was longing for the past and it was something Tom and I did it together, or is it part of who I am now in this new life? With at least seventy-five people in his lecture and only twenty spots on the trip surely the sheet was full, but I could not leave without checking.

"Is the sheet full?" I asked.

"No!" said the attendant motioning me over. "Join up."

Excited and nervous I added my name to the list, which was only half full. I had taken the step. Would I be sorry? Would I spend six hours reminiscing about Tom, stuck in the past, aching for him?

The bus pulled out right on schedule. When I saw the first stream and heard water rushing over the rocks, I thought of how Tom stopped for pictures. I did miss him, but at the same time I knew that this was part of my new life. Cades Cove was part of my life with Tom, but it had also passed the test and remained a part of me. It was a good day.

❧ ❧

Perhaps the hardest part of grief is acceptance. We have been shaken by the loss and forever changed. In *A Grief Observed*, C.S. Lewis compared losing a mate to the amputation of a leg.

> *"To say the patient is 'getting over it' after the operation for appendicitis is one thing; after he's had his leg off it is quite another. After that operation either the wounded stump heals or the man dies. If it heals, the fierce, continuous pain will stop. Presently he'll get back his strength and be able to stump about on his wooden leg. He has 'got over it.' But he will probably have recurrent pains in the stump all his life, and perhaps pretty bad ones; and he will always be a one-legged man. There will be hardly any moment when he forgets it. Bathing, dressing, sitting down, and getting up again, even lying in bed, will all be different. His whole way of life will be changed. All sorts of pleasures and activities that he once took for granted will have to be simply written off. Duties too. At present*

I am learning to get about on crutches. Perhaps I shall presently be given a wooden leg. But I shall never be biped again."[10]

Without Tom life will never be as I planned, and yet I cannot succumb to the urge to give up and allow fear to hold me prisoner in grief. So I take another step through the darkness, and then all of a sudden a door ahead is ajar and a light pierces the endless night. There's a smile, a touch, a laugh. Pieces of the new life God still has planned for me begin to come together. There's a place on the bus for me.

Afterword

Don't try to manage the grief alone. Let people help you. When the pain overwhelms you, call someone. If a friend invites you to go somewhere, go. Join a Grief Support Group where you can be free to share your feelings openly with others experiencing the same emotions. The world is full of grieving people, and the greatest comfort comes from those who have been there and understand. I felt an instant bond with two widows in my group, and we remain close friends.

Keep a journal. Writing my thoughts down seemed to release the pain for a while. Don't worry about format or spelling, just write what you feel.

Make a scrapbook. Pictures helped me to remember happy times with Tom because as they told the story of our life together. After organizing the photos in chronological order, I jotted a brief note beside each one as I placed it on the page. Now when I miss Tom most I open the scrapbook and find comfort.

Try new things...

At a friend's insistence I joined a quilting class. To my surprise I found my niche, and now we meet once a week to work on our latest quilt.

Eventually, and almost against my will, I began little by little to piece together my new life. I had no choice. I did not want a new life. I was content with the one I had, but that door was closed. I couldn't go back. All I could do was put one foot in front of the other, open the door, and take a step.

Helpful Resources

Books:

A Grief Observed by C. S. Lewis
Shadowlands by C. S. Lewis
The Problem of Pain by C. S. Lewis
The Four Loves by C. S. Lewis
Don't Take My Grief Away by Doug Manning
One Minute After You Die by Erwin Lutzer
90 Minutes in Heaven by Don Piper
When Bad Things Happen to Good People by Rabbi Kushner
Learning to Breathe Again by Tammy Trent
The Year of Magical Thinking by Joan Didion
Meditations on Grief by Martha Whitmore Hickman

కేళి

Movies

Shadowlands – The story of C. S. Lewis and the loss of his wife

Dying Young—A young man faces death from cancer

P.S. I Love You – A young widow grieves her husband's death from a brain tumor

Reign Over Me – Man stuck in grief after losing his wife and children in 9/11 attack

Bonneville – A widow takes a road trip with two friends to scatter husband's ashes

Endnotes

1   *One Minute After You Die* by Erwin W. Lutzer, Oasis Audio under arrangement with Moody Press, 2003

2   *When Bad Things Happen to Good People*, by Harold S. Kushner, Random House Audiobooks, 1987

3   *To Where You Are* from Josh Groban CD, produced and arranged by Richard Marx; Reprise Records Warner Music Group, 2001

4   *Success*, Bessie Stanley, published in the Lincoln (Kansas) Sentinel 11/30/1905

5   *Word of God Speak*, by Mercy Me, produced by Peter Kipley, 2002

6   *Thank You, from Moments For The Heart*, Ray Boltz Music, Inc., 1992

7   *Go Light Your World*, sung by Kathy Troccoli from Songs 4 Life, Time Life Music, 1998

8   *Here I Am Lord*, Dan Schutte, 1991

9   *I Was There to Hear Your Borning Cry*, composed by John Ylvisaker, arranged by John Helgen,

published by Neil A. Kjos Music Company, 1996

10   *A Grief Observed*, by C. S. Lewis, HarperCollins Publishers, Inc. 2001, 52-53